TURN THE BATTLE AT THE GATE

An End-Time Battle Strategy

By NANCY KAPLAN

Turn the Battle at the Gate
An End-Time Battle Strategy
by Nancy Kaplan

Printed in the United States of America.

ISBN 9781498491693

Unless otherwise indicated, Scripture quotations taken from the New American Standard Bible (NASB). Copyright © 1960, 1962, 1963, 1968, 1971, 1972, 1973, 1975, 1977, 1995 by The Lockman Foundation. Used by permission. All rights reserved.

Scripture quotations taken from the King James Version (KJV) – *public domain*.

Scripture quotations taken from the New King James Version (NKJV). Copyright © 1982 by Thomas Nelson, Inc. Used by permission. All rights reserved.

www.xulonpress.com

TABLE OF CONTENTS

DEDICATION

T his book is dedicated to all of the hidden ones who have laid their lives down to intercede for the Kingdom of God to manifest on earth as it is in heaven. You have paid a price in the secret place and your reward is great. You are not unnoticed by the King of Glory. When He called, you answered. Where he led, you followed. When you reminded him of his word through declarations and proclamations, he watched over his word to perform it! He has heard your prayers and supplications for the lost, and accepted the sacrifice of your time, sleep, and strength. He has seen you weep, worship and dance before him, and his word to you is, "Well done good and faithful servant!" May the revelation in the following pages enhance your prayer life as you serve in the Army of the Living God, the God of Abraham, Isaac and Jacob, the King of Glory!

"The fear of the LORD tendeth to life:
and he that hath it shall abide satisfied;
he shall not be visited with evil."
(Prov. 19:23 KJV)

ACKNOWLEDGMENTS

First and foremost I would like to thank the King of Kings, for without the revelation from him on the strategy of "Going through the gates," the following pages would not have been recorded.

I would also like to express my sincere gratitude to Sarah Danor who spent many hours working tirelessly to edit this revision of *Weapons of Mass Deliverance*.

Thank you to Mary Lois Little, who oversees the End-Time Handmaidens in Jerusalem, for giving me the opportunity to teach the revelation at the House of Peace, Jerusalem.

Big thanks to Susan Bartlett, of Daystar Ministries International, Savannah, Georgia, for her encouragement, prayers and guidance in the publishing of the book.

I would also like to thank Monica Nagy of M&N Marketing Group for her professional expertise in rendering a cover which captures the essence of the material inside.

I will never forget the intercessors who have supported me in many ways. Milly Butler, Pat George, Daphne Lewis, Joni, Eliana, and Ruth, as well as Nancy Morgan of Daystar Ministries International, Savannah, Georgia thank you so much for your intercession and being there when I needed you!

Finally, I would like to thank you, the reader, for implementing this strategy in your sphere of influence so that you may "Turn the Battle at the Gate!"

FOREWORD

I first had the privilege of knowing Nancy Kaplan as a Bible teacher and then as a friend and author. For more than fifteen years I have been impressed with her rare combination of tremendous prophetic gifting and deep spirituality in the area of intercessory prayer. Both are given expression in this watershed volume on the gates from a Hebraic perspective. This work is certain to give rise to new reflections on strategies for intercessory prayer. In these critical days we must look at the forming army and how the LORD sees war, unity, prayer and positioning. As believers, we are grafted into the LORD's covenant plan with Abraham through Messiah. This book acts as a wake-up call to prayer warriors in the body of Messiah to stand and battle at "The Gates." Understanding the prophetic significance of the tribes of Israel is vital. That insight will help us advance the Lord's redemptive plan and facilitate HIS purposes in our own personal lives and territory. My prayer is that you will be as deeply moved as I was by this book and that you will see that it gets in the hands of pastors, Messianic leaders, and Christian believers across this globe.

Jennifer Scrivner, PhD.

Woodstock, Georgia

November 1, 2016

INTRODUCTION

D o we have time to turn the battle at the gate? How can a nation, founded on the principles of life, liberty and justice for all, turn around when laws have been enacted, and even celebrated, that will systematically and deliberately bring about that nation's demise? Have we not been warned by the King of the Universe?

'But if you do not obey Me and do not carry out all these commandments, if, instead, you reject My statutes, and if your soul abhors My ordinances so as not to carry out all My commandments, and so break My covenant, I, in turn, will do this to you: I will appoint over you a sudden terror, consumption and fever that will waste away the eyes and cause the soul to pine away; also, you will sow your seed uselessly, for your enemies will eat it up. I will set My face

against you so that you will be struck down before your enemies; and those who hate you will rule over you, and you will flee when no one is pursuing you. If also after these things you do not obey Me, then I will punish you seven times more for your sins. I will also break down your pride of power; I will also make your sky like iron and your earth like bronze. Your strength will be spent uselessly, for your land will not yield its produce and the trees of the land will not yield their fruit. (Lev. 26:14-20)

And further, "*If the foundations are destroyed, What can the righteous do?*" (Ps. 11:3)

I asked myself this question while musing over what I had seen on the internet earlier in the day. What I heard caused me to reflect on a revelation of a strategy in spiritual warfare that the Lord gave me in 1999, which I taught for many years. Now, about 17 years later, I had found myself watching *The Jim Baker Show* and his guest was Michael Snyder who writes *The Economic Collapse* blog and who had recently authored the book *Rapture Verdict*. Michael was sharing on Israel and, specifically, about how God still cares about the city of Jerusalem and his people. He then quoted Revelation 21:10-13

And he carried me away in the Spirit to a great and high mountain, and showed me the Holy City, Jerusalem, descending out of heaven from God, having the glory of God, her light like a most precious jewel, like a jasper, clear as crystal. It had a great, high wall, with twelve gates, and at the gates twelve angels, and on the gates the names of the twelve tribes of the sons of Israel were written: three gates on the east, three gates on the north, three gates on the south, and three gates on the west. (Rev. 21:10-13)

Michael discussed dividing up God's land and the ominous results and retribution that would be suffered if this division takes place. He noted that the Lord had not forgotten Israel as he had even named the gates of the city after the 12 tribes of Israel. (Snyder 2016) Mr. Snyder was saying more than he may even have realized. This last statement mirrors the revelation the Lord gave me about the gates which became a strategy in spiritual warfare.

While the panel discussed the difficult times we are living in and contemporary problems, Jim Bakker's wife Lori asked, "Now what can we do? We need to know the solution. What is the solution?" Someone in the audience shouted, "We can pray!"

The Lord had recently impressed on my heart that he would lead me by his eye. (Ps. 32:8 NKJV) As I watched the program, I realized he was leading me to revisit the strategy he had given me years before. He encouraged me with an answer to the question I was pondering, based on Isaiah 28:5-6. Could the battle be turned at the gate?

> *In that day the Lord of hosts will be*
> *For a crown of glory and a diadem of beauty*
> *To the remnant of His people,*
> *For a spirit of justice to him who sits in judgment,*
> *And for strength to those who turn back the battle*
> *at the gate.*
> (Isa.28:5-6 NKJV)

From Revelation 21:10-13 (referenced above), the Lord had revealed to me in 1999 that there was a relationship between the names of the tribes on the gates and the strongholds. This understanding unlocked a much needed powerful prayer strategy for spiritual warfare. We certainly need every strategy that the Holy Spirit puts at our disposal. It seems as if the good news of the gospel is being crowded out at warp speed by what we see and hear going on these days, many of them warning signs from God's Word of what would happen in these last days.

> There will be signs in sun and moon and stars, and on the earth dismay among nations, in perplexity at the roaring of the sea and the waves, men fainting from fear and the expectation of the things which are coming upon the world; for the powers of the heavens will be shaken. Then they will see the Son of Man coming in a cloud with power and great glory. But when these things begin to take place, straighten up and lift up your heads, because your redemption is drawing near." (Luke 21:25-28)

With what is happening in our world today we all should have a crick in our neck from looking up! How appropriate, then, that I first shared the revelation of this prayer strategy in 1999, in Yulee, Florida, at a street ministry called Hope House. The one thing needed these days for the body of Messiah and the world is hope.

My understanding of the revelation on the gates has been expanded and deepened over the years. It started out as an extended outline consisting of 33 pages and became a book called *Weapons of Mass Deliverance*, which was published in June 2004.

When I first began sharing this revelation 17 years ago, I was teaching a group of about 60 intercessors in the home of a friend in Orange Park, Florida. After hearing the teaching my friend said, "This is an end time revelation!" The time is short to distribute, teach and impart this end-time strategy in order to equip and encourage prayer warriors to implement it. In the following pages I will share the original revelation, as well as the insights I have gained and gleaned over the years. It is my hope that we as one body, one mind and one spirit will be empowered by the Spirit of the living God to turn the battle at the gate in our lives, families, neighborhoods, cities and possibly even our nation.

As you read this book, ask the Holy Spirit to teach you how to pray at the gates and to anoint you to pray so that your prayers will become fervent and effectual and not a legalistic exercise which will produce little, if any, fruit. Then it will become a tool in your hand that the Holy Spirit can use to lead, guide and quicken you to pray effectively for yourself, your family, your city and your nation. The keys you are being given must be used in order to benefit you and those for whom you are standing in the gap.

Much of what you will read is a revised version of *Weapons of Mass Deliverance*. The foundation is the same, but this time multi-dimensional aspects of praying at the gates are brought to light. As you read through the book you will find yourself learning a strategy, but you may also discover yourself living inside of the gate of God's glory! Be blessed as you continue your journey into the unknown.

Chapter 1

KEEPER OF THE GATE

You, dear reader, are a gatekeeper. Whether you like it or not, know it or not, believe it or not, receive it or not, you, indeed, are a gatekeeper. Now don't misunderstand me, you are much more than a gatekeeper. In fact, you are more than a conqueror through him who loved you. Nevertheless, you have responsibilities and privileges as a gatekeeper. When exercising your authority, you establish the Kingdom of God (that is the God of Abraham, Isaac and Jacob) as he so directs you.

Recently, just before I was going to address a group of women regarding this teaching, a friend said to me, "You are just an antenna. Just receive what the Lord is saying and let it flow through you." I agreed to a certain point, but inside I knew in the natural that my frame had nothing in common with an antenna, not to mention that the word "antenna" is not even in scripture! Something inside of me rose up and my inner voice protested. The Word of God began to surface and I found myself countering the notion that "you are only an antenna" with phrases like: "I am a child of God, the bride of Messiah, beloved, accepted, chosen, more than a conqueror through him who loved me." It was evident I was taking every thought captive to the obedience of Messiah. Was this pride or arrogance or was this the gatekeeper inside guarding the gate? After all, *"For as he thinks within himself, so he is."* (Prov. 23:7)

The word sha'ar in Hebrew means gate. *Strong's Exhaustive Concordance of the Bible* word number H8179 matches the Hebrew שַׁעַר (*sha`ar*), which occurs 371 times in 302 verses in the King James Version of the Bible. The definition of 8179 is: gate

1 gate (of entrance)
2 gate (of space inside gate, i.e. marketplace, public meeting place, city, town)
3 gate (of palace, royal castle, temple, court of tabernacle)
4 heaven

Did you know that the same word "sha'ar" in Hebrew in the verb form means "thinks?" This definition of gate in the verb form only occurs one time in scripture. It occurs in

Proverbs 23:7 (referenced above). Now let's look at the verb form which is 8176 in the Hebrew concordance. Here is the definition in the Blue Letter Bible:

To split open, reason out, calculate (Prov. 23:7), reckon, estimate; to cleave, to divide, to open in fissures. (Strong n.d.)

Think of a brain. Does it not have fissures? Are we not called to divide the Word of God rightly? *"Do your best to present yourself to God as one approved, a worker who does not need to be ashamed and who correctly handles the word of truth."* (2 Tim. 2:15) So Proverbs 23:7 literally means, *"For as he **gates** within himself, so he is."* They are interchangeable. As a man "gates" or thinks in his heart, so is he.

A gate in scripture represents a seat of authority. Who sits on the throne in your "gate" (mind and thoughts) or seat of authority? Answer: Whoever you surrender to.

Yeshua (Jesus) is a gate! He says no one comes to the Father but through me: *"Jesus said to him, "I am the way, and the truth, and the life; no one comes to the Father but through Me."* (John 14:6)

Do you think you have the power to change your situation? Do you take the authority that has been given to you by the Almighty? Are you more or less than a conqueror through him who loved you? How do you "gate" in your heart? When you declare a thing, is it established in

23

your "gate" or mind? Do you waiver? Do you believe it is established?

Psalm 87:2 states, *"The Lord loves the gates of Zion more than all the dwelling places of Jacob."* A gate – or a door – swings two ways. In order for us to enter into God's presence, we must go through Yeshua to get to the Father. Yeshua is the only way to the Father. (John 14:6) Once we have come into the Father's presence, he is able to move through us – to touch the lost, the oppressed and the dying of our generation. As the gatekeepers, worshipers, musicians, dancers and prophetic intercessors praise God, he inhabits their praise. As they go through Messiah into the Father, the Father goes through them into the world. As these called, chosen, beloved and accepted gatekeepers and worshippers exercise their authority at the gates, the enemy is defeated and God is exalted!

Yeshua has also been given all authority and he has given that authority to you and me. *"Behold, I have given you authority to tread on serpents and scorpions, and over all the power of the enemy, and nothing will injure you."* (Luke 10:19)

We have the power to exercise the authority God has given us. We can either come into agreement with what is written in scripture or we can abdicate our authority and receive whatever the destroyer decides to throw our way.

It is our choice as a gatekeeper. We can choose to accept or reject love, truth, light, wisdom, understanding, healing, counsel, grace, mercy, favor and so on.

> *"If it is disagreeable in your sight to serve the LORD, choose for yourselves today whom you will serve: whether the gods which your fathers served which were beyond the River, or the gods of the Amorites in whose land you are living; but as for me and my house, we will serve the LORD."* (Josh. 24:15)

In 2016, a highly demonic event out of Belgium called "Tomorrowland" was to be live-streamed to a number of nations simultaneously, including Israel. It was scheduled to be broadcast at the arena in Jerusalem. Before the event, I was at a 24/7 prayer and worship ministry in Jerusalem and we were praying that the enemy would not breach the walls of Jerusalem through this event. One young Israeli man at this prayer meeting prayed fervently and effectively that the gates of the city would be marked with the blood of Yeshua. I got very excited as he prayed this because, whether he realized it or not, he was praying that the minds (thoughts, "gates") of those in this city would be marked with the blood of the Messiah. The curses that were intended to capture the minds of the young people in this nation were restrained by a prayer warrior in this meeting who, by the Spirit, called upon the Lord of Hosts to mark the gates (minds) of the youth and the residents in the city of our King with the blood of the Lamb.

Much prayer went up from intercessory prayer networks around the world and, fortunately, in Israel, the event turned out to be a total flop. Not many attended, the satellite feed was interrupted, and it was evident that God heard and answered the prayers of his people. The gatekeepers here and around the world engaged in the battle as the Lord, by his Spirit, led them to exercise their authority and pray strategically, which resulted in turning the battle at the gate! Praise the Lord!

Let's journey to Egypt for a brief moment. Remember, the Lord had the children of Israel put the blood of the lamb on the doorposts or gates of their homes. When judgement fell, the Angel of Death passed over the homes of those who had the blood on their doorposts/gates. In this case, the blood was applied to the actual entrances of their homes. A symbolic act of obedience saved a people and a future nation. Whether the blood of a lamb was physically applied to the doorposts of Israeli homes in Egypt or the blood of Yeshua is applied to our minds through speaking, the redemptive key of the blood restrains the curse. Hallelujah!

When Yeshua was brought before Pilate:

Pilate said to them, "Then what shall I do with Jesus who is called Christ?" They all said, "Crucify Him!" And he said, "Why, what evil has He done?" But they kept shouting all the more, saying, "Crucify Him!" When Pilate saw that he was accomplishing nothing, but rather that a riot was starting, he took water and washed his hands in front of the crowd, saying, "I am innocent of this Man's blood; see to that your-selves." And all the people said, "His blood shall be on us and on our children!" (Matt. 27: 22-25)

While the people's words were actually a self-invoked curse, they were, in fact, speaking prophetically about the innocent blood of Yeshua being on them for redemption. This invocation has actually preserved the people and the nation to this very day! Selah!

Isaiah 28:5-6 declares: *"In that day the Lord of Hosts shall become... a spirit of justice for him who sits in judgment, and strength to those who turn away the battle at the gate."* (Modern English Version, MEV)

Again I asked the Lord, "Do we have time to turn the battle at the gate for ourselves, our families, our cities and nations?"

Many years ago the Lord opened doors for me to teach on the gates in Maryland. While I was there, I stayed at the home of an apostle with whom I had a very edifying relationship. As I was walking around her neighborhood, the Lord asked me, "Nancy, where are you?" I answered, "I am in Howard County, Maryland, Lord." He asked me again, "Nancy, where are you?" I answered a little louder, "I am in Howard County, Maryland, Lord." He asked me a third time, "Nancy, where are you?" I was getting a little irritated but persisted, "I am in Howard County, Maryland, Lord!" My response at this point was audibly louder and emphatic. When he asked me the fourth time, it occurred to me that I had better think about the answer, because the answer I was giving to him was obviously incorrect. After thinking for a couple of minutes I said, "I am seated with Christ in heavenly places." At that point, he stopped asking me that question.

We are being trained to rule and reign with Messiah. Therefore, it is important to renew our minds (gates) with a few pertinent scriptures. Two of the following scriptures have the address "24:7." Hmm... could that possibly refer to 24 hours a day, seven days a week, around the clock prayer without ceasing? Psalm 24:7 and Proverbs 24:7... read, declare, meditate on and understand them!

> *Lift up your heads, O gates, and be lifted up, O ancient doors, that the King of glory may come in! Who is the King of glory? The Lord strong and mighty, The Lord mighty in battle. Lift up your heads, O gates, and lift them up, O ancient doors, that the King of glory may come in! Who is this King of glory? The Lord of hosts, He is the King of glory. Selah.* (Ps. 24:7-10)

As you meditate on this scripture, consider this question: How does a gate lift up its head? Let me give you an illustration. When you lift up your arms or legs and repeat the motion, you are exercising, are you not? Since a gate is a seat of authority and you are a gate, you are, therefore, a seat of authority! "Lift up your heads O gates" means **exercise your authority**!

Our authority comes from the Most High. *"And He called the twelve together, and gave them power and authority over all the demons, and to heal diseases."* (Luke 9:1) The verse comes alive with, *"Lift up your heads O ye gates..."* meaning exercise your authority!

Now let's look at Proverbs 24:7. *"Wisdom is too exalted for a fool, he does not open his mouth in the gate."* (Prov. 24:7) Here we see that if we are not to be called fools, we should open our mouths at the gate.

> *"Like arrows in the hand of a warrior, so are the children of one's youth. How blessed is the man whose quiver is full of them; They will not be ashamed when they speak with their enemies in the gate."* (Ps 127:4-5)

> *"Heed instruction and be wise, and do not neglect it. Blessed is the man who listens to me, watching daily at my gates, waiting at my door-posts. For he who finds me finds life and obtains favor from the Lord."* (Prov. 8:33-35)

Let's look at a few scriptures and answer the question of why we should be exercising our God-given authority. As you read these scriptures, ask the Holy Spirit if you have abdicated your God-given authority regarding yourself, your family, your city, congregation or nation.

"Now the Lord is the Spirit. And where the Spirit of the Lord is, there is liberty." (2 Cor. 3:17) That's a good reason to exercise our authority. Who wants to live in bondage?

"The evil bow before the good, and the wicked at the gates (authority) of the righteous." (Prov. 14:19) Something must be wrong with the images we are seeing daily on our computers and television screens! Could it be that we have not been exercising the authority we have been given, and this is the result?

> *"Yeshua said, 'I also say to you that you are Peter, and upon this rock I will build My church; and the gates of Hades will not overpower it.'"* (Matt. 16:18)

Chapter 2

GO THROUGH THE GATES

The Lord began to open up to me the prayer strategy of praying at the gates as I was lying in bed totally downcast, defeated, worn out, and over it. The words I heard him speak were, "Go through, go through the gates!" I knew the scripture had something to do with intercession but did not have the full understanding of what he was going to reveal. As he downloaded the teaching, hope began to rise, at least enough to get me out of bed and on my feet again.

The scripture found in Isaiah 62:10-12 became the starting point of discovery as the Lord began to open up my understanding of what it really means to "Go through, go through the gates!" Listen to what God is saying through the prophet Isaiah:

Go through, go through the gates, Clear the way for the people; Build up, build up the highway, Remove the stones, lift up a standard over the peoples. Behold, the Lord has proclaimed to the end of the earth, Say to the daughter of Zion, Lo, your salvation comes; Behold His reward is with Him, and His recompense before Him. And they will call them, "The holy people, the redeemed of the Lord"; And you will be called, "Sought out, a city not forsaken." (Isa. 62:10-12)

"Go through, go through the gates..." "Go" is an imperative. Imperative means essential, necessary, crucial, critical and important. Therefore, to God it is essential, necessary, important, crucial and critical to go through the gates. He even has Isaiah say it twice. "Go" is an order. "Go" is a command. "Go" is a call to action. "Go through the gates." There is more than one gate and the command is to go through the gates. Clear the way for the unsaved peoples. We are commanded to clear the way for the peoples to come to the Lord.

Clear the way for the Lord in the wilderness and build up a highway for the Holy Spirit. The Holy Spirit wants a highway of holiness. The unclean will not walk there. Let's think about that for a moment. What is a highway? The basic purpose and function of a highway is to allow you to get from one place to another quickly. A highway doesn't have any detours. A highway doesn't have any traffic lights. A highway doesn't have any stop signs. Highways are constructed to eliminate delays and allow you to move — *fast!* Right? With that in mind, listen to what God is saying. *"...Clear the way for the people; Build up, build up the highway, Remove the stones, lift up a standard over the peoples. Behold, the Lord has proclaimed to the end of the earth, Say to the daughter of Zion, 'Lo, your salvation comes; Behold His reward is with Him.'"* (Isa. 62:10-11) The Hebrew word for "salvation" here is "yeshua," Jesus' name in Hebrew. Your Yeshua/Jesus is coming! The reward is Yeshua! The reward is God, himself, but we need to clear the way and open up the highway so the world can see him and come to him. When we read this text from Isaiah, we see that we are commanded to go through the gates. We're commanded to build up a highway. We're commanded to remove the stones and to clear the way for the Lord in the wilderness.

You'll notice when you read the Bible, that most scriptures have a "mate." By that I mean a verse that is similar and acts as a confirmation. According to the Word of God, everything is confirmed in the mouth of at least two witnesses. *"But if he does not listen to you, take one or two more with you, so that by the mouth of two or three witnesses every fact may be confirmed."* (Matt. 18:16) Having said that, let's look at this "mate" scripture in Isaiah 40:3-5.

> *A voice is calling, "Clear the way for the Lord in the wilderness; Make smooth in the desert a highway for our God. Let every valley be lifted up, and every mountain and hill be made low; and let the rough ground become a plain, and the rugged terrain a broad valley; Then the glory of the Lord will be revealed, And all flesh will see it together; For the mouth of the Lord has spoken."* (Isa. 40:3-5)

"A voice is calling, 'Clear the way for the Lord in the wilderness.'" Does that sound familiar? *"Make smooth in the desert a highway for our God."* There's that highway again. *"Let every valley be lifted up and every mountain and hill be made low; and let the rough ground become a plain and the rugged terrain a broad valley."* Now look at the next word... **Then.** *"****Then** the glory of the Lord will be revealed, and all flesh will see it together; for the mouth of the Lord has spoken."* The glory of the Lord will come *after* we clear the way for the Lord in the wilderness. Make a highway! There are certain things that must be done through intercession before the glory of the Lord is revealed. Isaiah gives

us keys to what those things are. One key, found in Isaiah 62:10, has to do with "stones." We must remove the stones. What do stones represent in the Bible? Stones represent hard hearts. Before we address the heart issues, scripture is very clear that we enter his gates with thanksgiving and his courts with praise!

> *Praise the Lord! Sing to the Lord a new song, And His praise in the congregation of the godly ones. Let Israel be glad in his Maker; Let the sons of Zion rejoice in their King. Let them praise His name with dancing; Let them sing praises to Him with timbrel and lyre. For the Lord takes pleasure in His people; He will beautify the afflicted ones with salvation. Let the godly ones exult in glory; Let them sing for joy on their beds. Let the high praises of God be in their mouth, and a two-edged sword in their hand, to execute vengeance on the nations and punishment on the peoples, to bind their kings with chains and their nobles with fetters of iron, to execute on them the judgment written; This is an honor for all His godly ones. Praise the Lord! (Ps. 149)*

The text above from Psalm 149 really makes it clear to us that those who praise His name through dance, song and instruments are able to execute vengeance, binding kings and nobles — restraining strongholds, principalities and powers — with chains and fetters of iron. AMEN! When the worshipers, musicians, dancers and intercessors unite together, they become a formidable force in entering the presence of God, piercing through the darkness in the heavenlies, and allowing the Shekinah glory of God to come through to the earth. The power of these worshippers and intercessors uniting can impact multitudes in cities and nations – allowing people everywhere to come to the saving knowledge of the Most High God.

If you are praising and worshipping with all of your heart, you are a weapon of mass deliverance. As I write this, many on the internet have been talking about martial law being ordered in the USA. Many are expecting and seeing riots, terrorism, chaos... you name it. We have all heard and, unfortunately, seen the reports. Let me share with you part of a journal entry I wrote in 2014 before these predictions became so prevalent. I believe it will encourage you to praise and worship even more than you do. *The gates of each city will be opened or closed determined by the praise and worship of those [the believers in the city] and the level of worship and praise they engage in.* Based on what we have learned regarding gates so far, we can examine this entry in the light we have. The gates of the city can represent actual access points in and out of the city such as seaports, airports, roads, highways, bridges and tunnels. To whom will access be granted or denied? It may depend on our worship since where the Spirit of the Lord is, there is liberty! We have all taken for granted our ability to move freely. Dear God, may we never lose that freedom! The gates of each city can represent the authorities of that city (including governmental authorities) allowing or forbidding certain legislation, activities, events, building permits, or types of worship gatherings. The gates can also represent the minds and/or thought patterns of those who reside in the city, and whether or not they will be open to the gospel. You are called to be a gatekeeper, not only for yourself and your family, but as one who has been given authority by the Sovereign Lord, whose desire is to work his will through you as you co-labor with him to establish his kingdom on earth as it is in heaven.

Truly I say to you, whatever you bind on earth shall have been bound in heaven; and whatever you loose on earth shall have been loosed in heaven. (Matt. 18:18) In other words, whatever you forbid will be forbidden and whatever you allow will be allowed. So if praise and worship according to Psalm 149 binds kings with chains and nobles with fetters of iron, I guess it's time to crank up the music, Myrtle!

Thank God for the youth who are on the right track (no pun intended) and moving in Holy Ghost power!

Question: Do you not have the right to exercise spiritual authority over your city and nation? Are you exercising the authority you possess or is your authority being usurped by the enemy simply because you have abdicated the right to exercise it? There is no condemnation in these questions, they are only to encourage those who have laid down their weapons of spiritual warfare.

In the midst of praise and worship, God himself covers our heads in the day of battle.

> *I said to the Lord, "You are my God; Give ear, O Lord, to the voice of my supplications. O God the Lord, the strength of my salvation, You have covered my head in the day of battle. Do not grant, O Lord, the desires of the wicked; Do not promote his evil device, that they not be exalted. Selah. As for the head of those who surround me, May the mischief of their lips cover them."* (Ps. 140:6-9)

> *In the morning, O Lord, You will hear my voice; In the morning I will order my prayer to You and eagerly watch. For You are not a God who takes*

pleasure in wickedness; No evil dwells with You. The boastful shall not stand before Your eyes; You hate all who do iniquity. You destroy those who speak falsehood; The Lord abhors the man of bloodshed and deceit. But as for me, by Your abundant lovingkindness I will enter Your house, At Your holy temple I will bow in reverence for You. (Ps. 5:3-7)

The Lord lives, and blessed be my rock; and exalted be the God of my salvation, The God who executes vengeance for me, and subdues peoples under me. He delivers me from my enemies; Surely You lift me above those who rise up against me; You rescue me from the violent man. Therefore I will give thanks to You among the nations, O Lord, and I will sing praises to Your name. (Ps. 18:46-49)

He who offers a sacrifice of thanksgiving honors Me; and to him who orders his way aright I shall show the salvation of God." (Ps. 50:23)

But as for me, I shall sing of Your strength; Yes, I shall joyfully sing of Your lovingkindness in the morning, For You have been my stronghold And a refuge in the day of my distress. O my strength, I will sing praises to You; For God is my stronghold, the God who shows me loving-kindness. (Ps. 59:16-17)

I asked the Holy Spirit to quicken this revelation to you. I pray that you see the strategy that God has for you to implement.

Twelve is a very key number. It represents governmental authority. There are 12 gates in the New Jerusalem, 12 tribes and 12 angels at the gates in the New Jerusalem. My prayer is that God would raise up groups of 12 intercessors all over the world to go through the gates! (Isa. 62:10-11) In fact, the King of Glory has chosen 12,000 from each of the 12 tribes (that is 144,000) to be sealed or protected from what is coming upon the earth!

After this I saw four angels standing at the four corners of the earth, holding back the four winds of the earth, so that no wind would blow on the earth or on the sea or on any tree. And I saw another angel ascending from the rising of the sun, having the seal of the living God; and he cried out with a loud voice to the four angels to whom it was granted to harm the earth and the sea, saying, "Do not harm the earth or the sea or the trees until we have sealed the bond-servants of our God on their foreheads. And I heard the number of those who were sealed, one hundred and forty-four thousand sealed from every tribe of the sons of Israel. (Rev. 7:1-4)

As you continue to read, you will learn more about the gates. You will understand what occurred at the gates and how that applies to your prayer life and intercession. You will also discover the following:

- How praying at the gates illuminates a pattern from Heaven;
- How timely and strategic interceding at the gates is;
- How you can bring heaven to earth in your city;
- How to cooperate with the Holy Spirit while praying at the gates;
- The significance of coupling intercession with Hebraic roots;
- Divine positioning.

It is my desire to share with you the power of what the Lord has revealed to me, but the next step depends on you!

Once you have the revelation and knowledge, you must take action by using the keys in this book and applying them in your times of intercession. I beseech each one of you to ask the Holy Spirit to teach you how he would have you go through the gates when you pray.

Chapter 3

WHAT IS ANTIMONY?

Issues of the Heart

"Moreover, I will give you a new heart and put a new spirit within you; and I will remove the heart of stone from your flesh and give you a heart of flesh." (Ezek. 36:26)

I sn't it a blessing to know that we have received a new heart? Out of his grace, God gave us a new heart; our responsibility is to keep it with all diligence. *"Watch over your heart with all diligence, for from it flow the springs of life."* (Prov. 4:23)

We have all had our wilderness experiences and stories. There is no sense in reopening old wounds and dwelling on the past unless the wounds have not been healed. I remember a time I was walking with my little dog Yofe in the streets of Jerusalem. I noticed he was limping and when I looked under his paw, I saw a stone was lodged in between the pads. (Actually, it was a piece of hard, sticky candy). I removed it. He was relieved and his gait was restored. So it is with us. We are walking with the Lord, all is well, and then along the way we pick up a little offense here, a little unforgiveness there, some pride here, an attitude there, a little murmuring here, some bitterness, doubt and unbelief there and, before you know it, your heart has become hardened because of the stones you've picked up along the way. I guess one irritation is when you are walking along and get a little gummy self-righteousness stuck to you! That certainly is a sticky wicket! These sins create wounds on our souls which give the enemy a legal right to afflict us.

"Oh, afflicted one, storm-tossed and not comforted. Behold I will set your stones in antimony." (Isa. 54:11) In some Bibles it says "fair colors" instead of "antimony." Then Isaiah continues, *"And your foundations I will lay in sapphires. Moreover, I will make your battlements of rubies, and your gates of crystal, and your entire wall of precious stones."* (Isa. 54:12) God's going to set our stones (or heart issues; wrong attitudes) in antimony. What's antimony? What does God mean when he says he'll set your stones in "antimony?"

There are certain "stones" in our lives, whether they are bitterness, anger, resentment, judgmental attitudes, old wounds, whatever they may be, that we confess and bring before God. Yet even after we confess them, somehow we do not get down to the root of the problem completely. The surface situation is taken care of, but the root problem is still there. God wants to exterminate the root. The reason he wants to exterminate the root of the problem is that he knows that unless he does, the fruit will be rotten. When he says he's going to set your stones in antimony, it means he's going to blast those things right out of your life!

I looked up the definition of antimony because I didn't have a clue what it was. Antimony is a trivalent or a pentavalent metalloid element that is commonly found in most forms of explosives. Well, that got me excited! "Penta" means five. "Tri" means three. "Valent" means having or adding a degree of power to a radical or an element. In other words, you're going to add the power of three to an element. The power of the Father, Son and Holy Spirit are going to be added to you to blast those stones out of your life. A three-strand cord cannot easily be broken according to scripture. (Eccl. 4:14) They have the power to go to the radical, to go to the element, to go to the deepest part and blast it out of your life. The other term is "Pentavalent." What is "penta?" "Penta" means "five." It's referring to the five-fold ministry:

the apostles, prophets, evangelists, teachers and pastors. God's going to use his five-fold ministry gifts to take out some stones! He's going to use those instruments of his to blast those stones out of your life. Why does God want to blast those stones out of your life? So the Holy Spirit can flow freely, enabling you to build up that highway that God can move through. God will take that wilderness that is in you and remove it, so that his presence and his glory can come through you. Then the glory of the Lord will come. When we're emptied out, then the glory of the Lord will come and all flesh will see it together, for the mouth of the Lord has spoken it. When we pray, we can remind God of his Word. "God, you said you would set my stones in antimony!" He's given us this promise.

Let's look at the next verse, Isaiah 54:12. What does it mean to lay your foundations in sapphires? Sapphires are gemstones of a blue color. Blue is associated with the anointing since we see in scripture that both the throne of God (Ezek. 1:26) and the ground beneath His feet (Exod. 24:10) are made from precious stones in radiant blue. Our foundation is going to be in the anointing. Our foundation is going to be in the presence of God! Old things have passed away and new things have come!

What does it mean to have battlements of rubies? Where are we going to battle from? Are we going to battle from a ruby? A ruby has a deep, red color. We're going to battle from the position of the blood of Messiah, which cleanses us of all iniquity. Hallelujah!

What about the crystal or carbuncle, as some translations call it? Your gates will be of crystal. The enemies attack at the gates. Your gates are transparent. Crystal is transparent. You'll be able to see the enemy. You'll know who the enemy is. *"For our struggle is not against flesh and blood, but against the rulers, against the powers, against the world forces of this darkness, against the spiritual forces of wickedness in the heavenly places."* (Eph. 6:12) You will see the spiritual enemy when he's coming. You won't look at the person. You'll look beyond the person. It may take some work to separate the person from the real enemy in the spirit — but God can get us there! Your gates will be of crystal and your entire wall will be of precious stone.

As God does this work in us, his glory will be revealed and everyone will see it!

> *"Let every valley be lifted up, and every mountain and hill be made low; And let the rough ground become a plain, and the rugged terrain a broad valley; Then the glory of the LORD will be revealed, and all flesh will see it together; For the mouth of the LORD has spoken."* (Is 40:4-5)

There are certain things that grieve the Holy Spirit and there are certain things that draw him closer. Speaking about the blood of Yeshua, singing about his blood, and having an understanding of his blood draws the Holy Spirit. Exalting Yeshua draws the Holy Spirit. Simply acknowledging the Holy Spirit draws him. However, if we decide to pick up some stones in our lives, we put him at a distance. He's not distancing himself permanently; he's just waiting until we repent so that he can be in fellowship with us. He never leaves us; we leave him.

> *Create in me a clean heart, O God, and renew a steadfast spirit within me. Do not cast me away from Your presence and do not take Your Holy Spirit from me. Restore to me the joy of Your salvation and sustain me with a willing spirit. Then I will teach transgressors Your ways and sinners will be converted to You. (Ps. 51:10-13)*

Chapter 4

A JOURNEY WITH MOSES

"Now the LORD said to Moses, Come up to Me on the mountain and remain there, and I will give you the stone tablets with the law and the commandment which I have written for their instruction." (Exod. 24:12)

The God of Abraham, Isaac and Jacob said to Moses, "Come up to the mountain and remain there." What did God do as a result of that time? He said, "I will give you stone tablets with the law and the commandments which I have written for the people's instruction." What did God give him? Stone tablets. What do stones represent? Hearts. God gave Moses his heart.

What is the law or teaching/instruction? It is Yeshua Ha Mashiach – Yeshua the anointed one or Messiah — the

Cornerstone. Remember, Yeshua came to fulfill the law. When God gave those two tablets to Moses, he gave him his heart. It was a glimpse into the future – a picture of Yeshua.

"Then Moses turned and went down from the mountain with the two tablets of the testimony in his hand, tablets which were written on both sides; they were written on one side and the other." (Exod. 32:15) Moses left the presence of God to return down the mountain and give the people God's heart. It took him 40 days, but God had given him his heart, which was the law — or his teaching and instruction. Basically, it was God's way of saying, "Follow my teachings and instructions and you will be blessed. Disregard my teachings and instructions, and you will be cursed."

Moses began the journey down the mountain to give the people God's heart. Let's take a look at what happened after that. *"And it came about, as soon as Moses came near the camp, that he saw the calf and the dancing; and Moses' anger burned and he threw the tablets from his hands and shattered them at the foot of the mountain."* (Exod. 32:19) Moses threw the tablets down, but more than the tablets got broken. It was a picture of God's heart being shattered. He symbolically broke God's heart. It broke God's heart to see the people moving into idolatry. God had just taken them out of Egypt. He had revealed himself through signs and wonders. He had parted the Red Sea. He had taken them out of slavery. Then, when he wanted to give them his heart, his law and his instruction, they broke his heart by going into idolatry! Now what is God going to do? His heart and his law or instruction have been broken.

"Now the LORD said to Moses," Cut out for yourself two *stone tablets like the former ones, and I will write on the tablets the words that were on the former tablets which you shattered."* (Exod. 34:1) The first time that Moses was on the mountain with God, God had already prepared the stone tablets and given them to Moses; but now he said, "Moses, you cut out two stone tablets for yourself."

Have you ever climbed a mountain? The air in higher altitudes is a lot lighter. It's harder to breathe. You get tired. Now, not only does Moses have to take himself up the mountain again, but he also has to cut two stone tablets. Do you know what that is giving us a picture of? It's a picture of intercession. When you intercede for people, you are the one who has to take the hearts of men to God. You're standing in the gap between God and man. You're taking those hearts up the mountain to God, asking him to write his law or teachings and instructions upon their hearts. It's work! You pay a price in intercession. You follow in the same footsteps as Moses.

"Behold, days are coming, declares the LORD, when I will make a new covenant with the

house of Israel and the house of Judah; not like
the covenant which I made with their fathers in
the day I took them by the hand to bring them
out of the land of Egypt. My covenant which
they broke, although I was a husband to them,
declares the Lord." (Jer. 31:31-32)

God was a husband to the Israelites when He took them out of the bondage of Egypt. He led them with a pillar of cloud by day and a pillar of fire by night. He kept them warm. He fed them. He took care of them. He protected them. He spared them from the Egyptians who were coming after them. He parted the Red Sea for them. He was a husband to them. He loved them, but they still broke his covenant. Do we ever break his covenants?

"But this is the covenant which I will make with
the house of Israel after those days, declares
the LORD, I'll put my law within them, and on
their heart I will write it; and I will be their God,
and they shall be My people. And they shall not
teach again, each man his neighbor and each
man his brother, saying, 'Know the LORD,' for
they shall all know Me, from the least of them
to the greatest of them, declares the LORD, for

I will forgive their iniquity, and their sin I will remember no more." (Jer. 31:33-34)

At first, God put the law on the stone tablets and gave it to Moses. Now he is saying, "I'm going to put my law within them and write it on their hearts." God is no longer going to write on the stone tablets. He's going to write on human hearts. God tells us, "I will be their God. They will be my people. I'll put Yeshua and my Spirit in them. Each man and his brother will know me." God's desire is to write his law or teachings and instruction upon our hearts.

What happens to us in intercession? When we start praying for others, we have got to make sure that the very things we're praying about for somebody else to be delivered from are not operating in us. Think about that for a moment. How can we pray something out of somebody else if it is in operation in us? God says that he is faithful and just to forgive us if we confess our sins. *"If we confess our sins, He is faithful and righteous to forgive us our sins and to cleanse us from all unrighteousness."* (1 John 1:9)

We cannot change ourselves. We can't change our own hearts. Only God can change our hearts. The first step requires us to acknowledge our sin. We can sit there and say, "Oh God, that person has so much pride. I just wish that you would deal with their pride." Maybe God wants to deal with your pride. To paraphrase Psalm 51, first, we need to earnestly say to God, "Change my heart. Create in me a clean heart. Renew a steadfast spirit within me. Don't cast me away from your Holy Spirit. Then I'll teach transgressors your ways and sinners shall be converted."

Let me talk about "stones" on a more personal level. As believers, the Lord has given us a heart transplant. He's taken out that heart of stone and he's put in a heart of flesh; however, as we go through life, things happen to us. The heart that he has given to us becomes a little hardened in spots. When we first got saved, we were on that glory ride, and the grass looked so much greener. Remember? We were in love with God and in love with everybody. Then six months passed, and God really began to show us the state of our hearts. We started feeling a little bit resentful towards certain things that happened to us. We may have felt a little anger or unforgiveness. Situations happened and we may have felt like we had a "right" to our emotions. We may have made statements like, "I choose to forgive them, God." If you confess your sins and repent, he deals with your stones.

Let me give you an illustration to help clarify this point. I was at a friend's house and I saw that she had a fish made out of hollow glass. We are like that fish. Usually, we have big mouths like fish! God tries to tame our tongue. A fish is the symbol of a Christian — and yet, some fish have many stones inside. When God first fills us with his Spirit, he doesn't have a whole lot of room to operate because we have all sorts of stones in the way. So, God starts talking to us about removing the bitterness, judgment, resentment and the critical spirit from our lives. In addition, there might be some smaller stones inside us that are a little harder to get out, like emotional wounds or disappointing things that happened to us over the course of our lives. Ultimately, God wants us to just flow with him.

Now, imagine that glass fish that I mentioned just a moment ago. If I put that fish loaded down with stones into the water, you know that it will stink – whoops! I mean sink. Get a picture of that in your mind. That fish is not going to move with the Spirit; it's not able to, because it's too weighted down. God wants to remove those stones! He's not going to remove them all at once. We wouldn't know what to do if he did that. He's going to take his time and reveal and unveil each stone. As you fast and pray, he loosens the bonds of wickedness in your life. He undoes the bands of the yoke. He lets the oppressed go free. He breaks every yoke while you fast and wait on him. Isaiah 58:6 says: *"Is this not the fast which I choose, to loosen the bonds of wickedness, to undo the bands of the yoke, and to let the oppressed go free, and break every yoke?"* As a result, you'll have more of a chance to swim a little bit. You will find that you have more freedom to allow the Holy Spirit to move through you.

I'd like to share a story about something that happened to me in Israel. At that time, I lived in Israel for exactly forty months. Forty is the number of testing and trials. I spent two years in Jerusalem in my own apartment, but the Lord was moving me to an area north of Tel Aviv. Before he moved me there, I went to the home of a friend who needed my help for a few weeks. I left my apartment. I left all my furnishings and my appliances with my roommate there, because she needed them.

I put my personal things in storage, except for my prized piano, which I loved. Instead I had given it to a friend I was going to help for a couple of weeks after she had surgery. Meanwhile, God already had confirmed to me that he had opened up a place for me north of Tel Aviv. I told this friend that I would come and help her while she recuperated during my last two weeks in Jerusalem. Near the end of those two weeks, I was doing a lot of schlepping. Do you know what "schlepping" means? It is a Yiddish word that means to carry or to lug something. I didn't have a car, so I either walked or rode the bus and schlepped whatever I needed to take with me in my hands. I knew she liked watermelon, and it happened to be the summer when watermelon was available. I would take a walk and schlep watermelons home for her.

So in addition to all that was necessary to take care of her while she was recovering, I would walk in very hot weather to schlep these watermelons for her.

Unfortunately, just a few days before it was time for me to go, we got into a conflict. I was doing my best to clean her house, cook for her, and take care of her, but I soon found out that she didn't like the way I was doing it. One day, she looked straight at me and insulted me using vulgar language, and said some very hurtful things. I thought to myself, "How demeaning! How degrading!" Can you imagine yourself in my position? Here I was trying to help her and she insulted me! I'll tell you, I think I added a few stones that day. I was angry and resentful. I was so upset that I took my dog and walked five miles back to the apartment that I'd just left two weeks before.

My former roommate had my $1,000.00 leather couch and my $800.00 dining room set and all of my appliances. She still had two empty bedrooms, so I explained to her what had happened and said, "I can't go back there." Much to my shock, she responded, "Well, you can't stay here!" Hold on a minute! She was using all of my appliances and furniture, yet when I turned to her in need, she said I couldn't stay there! I asked her, "Why?" She explained that she already had another roommate and they agreed that they wouldn't do anything unless they talked to each other first. The new roommate wasn't there and she didn't know how to get hold of her. I thought, "If I have to take one of my mattresses and bring it down these 54 stairs and sleep in the park downstairs on the outside of this building I'll do it, but I'm *not* going back to that house!"

So now, things were getting worse. More stones were being added. It was awful! I was really upset. I was angry and bitter and I had no idea what to do. I started walking again and I thought, "I have no place to go." I couldn't afford to go to a hotel so I headed over to the apartment of some people that I hadn't yet said good-bye to. By the time I got there, my former roommate called me, apologized and invited me to stay at her apartment, which I did for those last few days before I left for Tel Aviv. By the way, the other friend also apologized at a later date. Do you know that all of that happened in just a few hours of time?

The reason I told you that story is to show you that sometimes God puts us in certain situations to reveal what is really in our hearts. In the end, I had to forgive. At times, we're all capable of this kind of behavior. Sometimes, we're on the other side of the situation. We're the roommates that say, "No, you can't stay here." Sometimes we can be like the woman who used vulgar and insulting language. I'm sure many of you could identify with all the sides and personalities in that story. Through these types of situations,

God reveals what's in our own hearts. He wants to clean us up so we can flow with him. He really wants to blast those stones out of our lives completely!

Let's take a moment just to thank God. Father, we just thank you for this teaching. We pray that every stone would be removed out of our own hearts for your glory. We ask that you fill your temple with your presence, Lord. We welcome you, Holy Spirit. We ask you, Lord God, to take out of us all those things that are not pleasing to you. Reveal them to us. Cleanse your temple. Purify your temple, Father God. We offer you all the praise, all the glory, and all the honor. You are worthy of all praise. Thank you, God, that we can't do this in our own strength. We can only do all these things through you, who strengthens us. We glorify you and bless you Lord. We magnify your holy name. Make us that highway of holiness, in Yeshua's name, Amen.

Chapter 5

LAYING THE FOUNDATION

In the Old Testament there are many references to gates. For example, there were the Fish Gate, Sheep Gate, New Gate, Corner Gate, Water Gate, Horse Gate and Dung Gate. These gates and their names are symbols and shadows that correlate to events that occurred at those gates. Let's look at the symbolism of the gates.

The Sheep Gate

The Bible talks about the Sheep Gate in both the Tanakh and the Brit Chadasha (Old and New Testaments).

"Then Eliashib the high priest arose with his brothers the priests and built the Sheep Gate; they consecrated it and hung its doors." (Neh. 3:1) The name Eliashib means "God will restore." Right after I had moved from Israel back to

the USA, I had lost everything and it looked like nothing was working out, but God gave me ONE word – restore. In that moment, I needed to put my trust and hope in him and I was able to hang on to that one word, "Eliashib." It doesn't matter what you have lost, God will restore. If you haven't experienced full restoration, wait. It is coming. Be encouraged! God acts on behalf of those who wait for Him. (Isaiah 64:4).

> *"Now there is in Jerusalem by the Sheep Gate a pool, which is called in Hebrew Bethesda, having five porticoes."* (John 5:2)

> *"What man among you, if he has a hundred sheep and has lost one of them, does not leave the ninety-nine in the open pasture, and go after the one which is lost, until he finds it?"* (Luke 15:4)

We are the sheep of His pasture. Each of us is important to him. Nehemiah 3:1 tells us that the Sheep Gate was consecrated unto the Lord. If even one gets lost, He goes after that sheep until they are restored to the fold. Restoration comes at the Sheep Gate. It doesn't happen at the Water

Gate or at the High Gate of Benjamin. He restores at the Sheep Gate. That is where the sheep are restored.

The Inspection Gate/The Mustering Gate

The Bible also talks about the Inspection Gate or Mustering Gate, as it is also translated. *"After him Malkijah the goldsmith's son made repairs as far as the house of the temple servants and the merchants. This was across from the Mustering Gate extending as far as the upper room of the corner tower."* (Neh. 3:31 Modern English Version [MEV]) In the New American Standard Bible, the gate is referred to as the "Inspection Gate." Malkijah means "Jehovah is King." God our king inspects us and our lives. We can't hide from him. He knows where we are and what we are doing. He even knows our thoughts! He inspects our lives and he perfects everything that concerns us.

Now look with me at the definition of "mustering." When "muster" is used as a verb, it means to summon, call to arms, congregate or assemble. If there was ever a time for the troops to be mustered it is now! The word "muster" when used in the phrase "pass muster" means to be good enough, acceptable or adequate. Only because of the blood of the Lamb of God do we qualify. You are in the army now! Even if you've been on the shelf for a while and or in the reserves, you are being called up for duty. No more "at ease." No more do as you please.

> *"Arise, shine; for your light has come, and the glory of the Lord has risen upon you. For behold, darkness will cover the earth and deep darkness the peoples; But the Lord will rise upon you and His glory will appear upon you. Nations will come to your light, and kings to the brightness of your rising."* (Isa. 60:1-3)

Both translations "inspection" and "muster" illuminate the significance of this gate as a place for God the King to rally his troops for the battle.

The Valley Gate

Next let's talk about the Valley Gate. *"Moreover, Uzziah built towers in Jerusalem at the Corner Gate and at the Valley Gate and at the corner buttress and fortified them."* (2 Chron. 26:9) Uzziah means "my strength is Jehovah." When we are going through the valley, Jehovah is our strength. When we are going through those times when we do not see God, feel God, hear God, and don't even think He is there, He is still carrying us. He is our strength.

The Water Gate

Now let's look at the Water Gate. The Water Gate is a place where the scriptures were read. Isn't it interesting that Ephesians 5:26 talks about the washing of the water of the word? The Water Gate was not the gate where the sheep were watered, rather it was the gate where the Word of God was read. *"He read from it before the square which was in front of the Water Gate from early morning until midday, in the presence of men and women, those who could under-stand; and all the people were attentive to the book of the law."* (Neh. 8:3) They were attentive to the Book of the Law. Where did this occur? Not at the Inspection Gate. Not at the Valley Gate. It happened at the Water Gate. Again, I want to emphasize the symbolism of these gates. Understand that they are only a shadow and a type. The Word of God was read at the Water Gate.

The Horse Gate

The Bible also talks about the Horse Gate. *"So they seized her, and when she arrived at the entrance of the Horse Gate of the king's house, they put her to death there."* (2 Chron. 23:15)

You die at the horse gate. Well, why would you die there? Why wouldn't you die at the water gate? Water — or the Word of God — brings life. *"The king is not saved by a mighty army; a warrior is not delivered by great strength. A horse is a false hope for victory; nor does it deliver anyone by its great strength."* (Ps. 33:16-17) So here we see death at the Horse Gate. You can't put your trust in horses. It will only lead to death. *"Some trust in chariots, and some in horses, but we will remember the name of the Lord our God."* (Ps. 20:7 MEV) So we see there that we can't put our trust or hope in the strength of a horse, or in the flesh. God wants us to depend on him so that he can live through us. We need to put our trust in the Name of the LORD and not our own abilities.

The Old Gate

The Bible mentions the Old Gate. *"Joiada the son of Paseah and Meshullam the son of Besodeiah repaired the Old Gate; they laid its beams and hung its doors with its bolts and its bars."* (Neh. 3:6) God wants to do a new thing at the Old Gate. The LORD made the old covenant, new.

> *"Behold, days are coming," declares the Lord,*
> *"when I will make a new covenant with the*
> *house of Israel and with the house of Judah,*

not like the covenant which I made with their fathers in the day I took them by the hand to bring them out of the land of Egypt, My covenant which they broke, although I was a husband to them," declares the Lord. "But this is the covenant which I will make with the house of Israel after those days," declares the Lord, "I will put My law within them and on their heart I will write it; and I will be their God, and they shall be My people." (Jer. 31:31-33)

In this new covenant, God wrote the law upon their hearts so that they would all know him. So, at the Old Gate we see that God wants to do something new in our lives. God is the Creator and he loves to do new things. He is not going to continue to repeat himself, and it is important to know that when it comes to intercession.

When I was in the middle of writing the second portion of the outline for my book, *Weapons of Mass Deliverance,* many people had asked me to write down prayers showing them how to go through the gates. At first, I didn't want to do it. Since God is so creative, I didn't want people to pray what the Holy Spirit was putting on my heart– I wanted them to pray what He was putting on their hearts. However, the Holy Spirit had me write prayers as examples, because there are times when it helps to have a model when learning a new concept. You will find those prayers in the back of that book. Keep in mind, however, that it's just an example. Ask God to show you how he wants you to pray at the gates.

I always ask God to teach me how to pray effectively at the gates. I ask him to tell me what is on his heart. As you pray, be sensitive to the Holy Spirit and let him reveal things to you. It is amazing what he will show you at the different gates and what he will put on your heart to pray. You need patience to wait and listen to what he is saying and then pray it back to him.

The Corner Gate

The same passage that mentions the Valley Gate in the Bible also talks about the Corner Gate. *"Moreover, Uzziah built towers in Jerusalem at the Corner Gate and at the Valley Gate and at the corner buttress and fortified them."* (2 Chron. 26:9) What does a corner represent? If I am walking and I end up at a corner, I can do one of two things: I have to go one way or the other. I can't go straight ahead. At a corner, a turn has to be made, so the Corner Gate represents repentance. You are turning. You are changing your mind. You are going in another direction. You also have to fortify that change in direction. In other words, if you are turning from evil, you have to fortify that in order to not go back to what you were involved with before you turned the corner. You need to strengthen or fortify that choice by not falling back into the sinful behavior.

The Dung Gate

The Bible tells us that one of Jerusalem's gates was known as the Dung Gate. I think that gate is self-explanatory. *"Therefore if anyone is in Christ, he is a new creature; the old things passed away; behold, new things have come."* (2 Cor. 5:17)

The Fountain Gate

Lastly we come to the Fountain Gate. *"Shallum the son of Col-hozeh, the official of the district of Mizpah, repaired the Fountain Gate."* (Neh. 3:15) Shallum built the Fountain Gate. Repair is taking place at the Fountain Gate. Yeshua made amends and atonement for us, so that we can have a fountain of life inside of us that will bubble up and move through us.

Chapter 6

WHERE WERE GATES FOUND IN BIBLICAL TIMES?

As I began to study and research information on gates, one of the first questions that came to mind was, "Where were gates found in the Bible?"

City Entrance

One of the places gates were found was at the entrance of a city. *"So he arose and went to Zarephath, and when he came to the gate of the city, behold, a widow was there gathering sticks."* (1 Kings 17:10)

Here in Revelation 21 we read that the New Jerusalem has a high wall, 12 city gates, 12 angels stationed at the gates, and the names of the gates were the 12 tribes of

Israel. This is a key scripture in praying at the gates and we will return to that a little bit later.

> *And he carried me away in the Spirit to a great and high mountain, and showed me the holy city, Jerusalem, coming down out of heaven from God, having the glory of God. Her brilliance was like a very costly stone, as a stone of crystal-clear jasper. It had a great and high wall, with twelve gates, and at the gates twelve angels; and names were written on them, which are the names of the twelve tribes of the sons of Israel. There were three gates on the east and three gates on the north and three gates on the south and three gates on the west.* (Rev. 21:10-13)

Isaiah 62:12 says, *"And they will call them, 'The holy people, the redeemed of the Lord'; and you will be called, 'Sought out, a city not forsaken.'"* (NASB) So as one of the redeemed of the Lord, *you* are called a city. Keep in mind that gates were found at the entrances to cities.

Houses

Gates were also found at houses. *"And a poor man named Lazarus was laid at his gate, covered with sores..."* (Luke 16:20) There is a story in Acts 12:14, where a servant girl named Rhoda recognized Peter's voice as he stood outside the gate knocking, but because of her joy, she did not open the gate. Instead she ran inside and announced that Peter was standing in front of the gate. So the gate was at the entrance of the house.

"...you also, as living stones, are being built up as a spiritual house for a holy priesthood, to offer up spiritual sacrifices acceptable to God through Jesus Christ." (1 Pet. 2:5) Just as you are called a "city not forsaken" in Isaiah 62:12, here in 1 Peter you are called a spiritual house. Gates were found at the entrances to cities and gates were also found at houses.

Temples

Gates were also found at temples. *"And a man who had been lame from his mother's womb was being carried along, whom they used to set down every day at the gate of the temple which is called Beautiful, in order to beg alms of those who were entering the temple."* (Acts 3:2) You are also called a temple in the epistles! *"Do you not know that you are a temple of God and that the Spirit of God dwells in you?"* (1 Cor. 3:16)

So far, we have seen that gates were found at the entrances of a city, at the entrance of a house and at the entrance of a temple. You are likened to a city, a house and a temple through the above examples in scripture. But there is more. Let's keep looking.

Palaces

Gates were found at palaces. In the book of Esther, verse 9 of chapter 5, Haman was seen sitting at the King's Gate. Wouldn't you love to enter the royal palace through the King's Gate? Again we see the King's Gate mentioned in verse 13, *"Yet all of this does not satisfy me every time I see Mordecai, the Jew, sitting at the king's gate."* (Esther 5:13)

Camps

Gates were also found at camps. *"Now when Moses saw that the people were out of control, for Aaron had let them get out of control to be a derision among their ene-mies— then Moses stood in the gate of the camp, and said, 'Whoever is for the Lord, come to me!'"* (Exod. 32:25-26)

Where was Moses standing? He was standing at the gate of the camp. Camps had gates.

Now camps in the Old Testament were gathering places for war. Do you realize that every day you are in a spiritual battle? Every day we have a choice. When we wake up, we can walk in the spirit or walk in the flesh and the choice is nothing short of a battle. So far we've seen that gates were found at houses, temples, palaces and entrances of cities. We are likened to three of those four things in that we are called a spiritual house, a temple and a city. Now we know that gates were found at camps and camps were gathering places for war, so guess what? It is time to make war with the enemy of our souls! You are the gatekeeper. Whatever you allow will be allowed, whatever you forbid will be forbidden!

Rivers

Scripture speaks of gates being found at rivers. *"The gates of the rivers are opened, and the palace is dissolved."* (Nahum 2:6) The Holy Spirit wants to flow like a river in and through our lives. When he begins to flow, the "palace" or the place of self-centeredness begins to dissolve. When we diminish, God increases. In addition, rivers represent the Holy Spirit and living waters. Yeshua likened the Holy Spirit to living waters when speaking to the woman at the well. *"If you knew the gift of God, and who it is who says to you, 'Give Me a drink', you would have asked Him, and He would have given you living water."* (John 4:10) And again, *"He who believes in me, as the Scripture said, 'From his innermost being shall flow rivers of living water.'"* (John 7:38) Also, *"There is a river whose streams make glad the city of God. The holy dwelling places of the Most High."* (Ps. 46:4)

Let's talk about the impact of yielding to the Holy Spirit for a moment. It's important to listen for his voice. The Lord may tell you to do some things that sound a little strange. He won't tell you to do something that would be contrary to the Word. When you hear his voice, just do it, obey. Many times we miss his voice because we do not recognize that the small impressions we get *are* actually his voice. Sometimes when we get impressions, we rationalize them away, talk ourselves out of doing what the Spirit is prompting us to do and get out of his flow. When we hear that still, small, quiet voice, it is critical to move on that impression. You will be amazed at how he will lead. Let me give you an example.

I was living in Israel in the mid 90's and was attending Ulpan, a Hebrew language course. I attended classes for five hours a day and it was very intense. If I missed one day of Ulpan, I missed a lot of material and had much to make up. One morning, on my way to Ulpan, the Holy Spirit gave me the impression not to attend classes that morning. I obeyed his voice even though it meant sacrificing a lot by missing a five hour day in Ulpan class. Instead, he directed me to do errands and walk around downtown Jerusalem. The entire time I was walking, I was praying and singing in the Spirit or in tongues. After a number of hours of doing that, on my way home I began to think this was a little bit nuts! That evening I asked the Lord, "Did that singing and praying do anything or make a difference in some way?" Here is what he showed me. That night, there was a terrorist attack in the area where I had been walking and praying. Tragically, two people were killed and 13 were wounded. However, because of the rain that night, not as many tourists were out as usual. The police found four grenades from which the pins had been pulled — but none of them had gone off! That's a miracle! Fifty people easily could have been killed if those grenades had gone off. The two terrorists who shot up and down the street were killed. Thank God for the lives that were spared! This all happened as a result of simple obedience to the voice or impression of the Holy Spirit.

Here is another example from my time living in Israel. A friend who lived in a different part of the country had come to visit for a couple of days. This friend wanted to talk with me, yet at the same time, the Spirit of the Lord had come upon me for the purpose of intercession. I was praying in tongues, so I motioned to her that I could not speak to her right then. Even though this was a friend, God had a hold of me and needed me at that moment. I needed to surrender to him so that he could accomplish what he wanted to do. It really doesn't matter what anybody else thinks, even though you may appear to be rude at times. You see, the Word declares, *"My sheep hear my voice ...and they follow me."* (John 10:27). I couldn't stop praying in tongues. After I was finished, I asked the Lord, "What was that all about?" He doesn't always tell you every time you ask, but on this occasion he spoke to me and said, "You just averted a terrorist attack." The next day, in the paper I read that a plot had been uncovered which entailed kidnapping the Mayor of Jerusalem and blowing up the Jerusalem Mall. The authorities apprehended these terrorists who were plotting this attack just before they could execute their insidious plot.

God wants to use us in these last days. The Word declares that we will do greater exploits than he did when he walked this earth. (John 14:12) The examples I am citing took place back in the 1990's. How much more today does he need us, our intercession and our obedience? Obviously, with the state the world is in today, he needs all hands on deck. It is imperative that we be willing and obedient to him when he calls. (Oy, I am sure I am going to be eating those words!) As you read these words, note that you are moving into a new place in him so that his glory can shine forth through you! Take courage, though, because it truly is no longer you that live but Messiah that lives in you! (Gal. 2:20) This is not a time to walk away from your post! (Isaiah 21:8) Stand still and see the salvation of God on your behalf. (2 Chron. 20:17)

There are so many examples of God's intervening power. If we would call upon his name and be sensitive to his voice and yield to his Spirit, there is no telling how he would use us.

There was another situation where I was shown that there was going to be a premature attack in the northern Galilee area and that it would involve poisonous gas. I told my pastor but I didn't have the funds to rent a car and go up to the northern Galilee to pray. That particular weekend, the Lord brought five intercessors from Brownsville Assembly of God in Pensacola, Florida to stay at his house. He did not share with them what the Lord had shown me, yet one of the visiting intercessors from Brownsville got the same warning about the attack in the northern Galilee. God showed them that if they went up there and prayed, the attack would be foiled. Those five intercessors went up to the northern Galilee and prayed that weekend and averted the terrorist attack by praying in unity. Again, *"My sheep hear my voice ... and they follow me."* (John 10:27) Some of the things the Holy Spirit reveals to us will not make sense to us in the natural world, but your job is only to hear the voice of the Holy

Spirit and follow him. *"...to obey is better than sacrifice..."* (1 Sam. 5:22)

One time I was in Haifa, Israel and the Lord only spoke one word to me. That word was London. "London?" I puzzled. "What do you mean?" When I returned to the USA after living in Israel, I met a man who happened to have an apartment in a predominantly Jewish part of London. God kept building on that. Once I was walking in a grocery store in a little town in Florida, and the Spirit of the Lord said, "Wait until you see who you are going to meet in the bakery section." I ended up meeting a couple from England. The Lord kept dropping little hints like those. Most of the time, God doesn't give us the whole picture. He gives us little impressions. That year, God sent me to London for intercession and I went with another lady. Little did we know that after we left London, three major evangelists would have meetings in England. Those three were Reinhardt Bonnke, Marilyn Hickey, and Roberts Liardon. They all had outreaches within weeks of one another. The reason we had been sent was now clear because before God will move in a particular area he will bring intercessors into that area. In fact, only after I returned to Florida, I discovered that another intercessor from my church accompanied her husband on a business trip to London at around the same time because the Lord impressed her to go along with him. While he was conducting business, she was attending to her Father's business.

Corporate prayer, which is praying together with other believers, is so powerful. If we come into unity with one another, God commands the blessing. (Ps. 133) When someone is leading out in prayer, support him or her and pray along with them. Think about standing at a gate with a battering ram. The battering ram is only going to be as strong as the manpower behind it. If you have 12 people holding onto that battering ram and using it to smash through the gate, you will be a lot more effective than one person trying to do it alone! Obviously, more people working together in unity produce more power. The different intercessors, musicians, dancers and worshippers, as well as those who declare the Word of the Lord, can unify corporately to go through a gate of a city. Do you see the power in that? Can you see God orchestrating his army to turn the battle at the gate? Individuals who come together corporately with a common goal under the leadership of the Holy Spirit can bind kings with chains and their nobles with fetters of iron — executing Psalm 149.

We have the privilege of yielding to the Holy Spirit's prompting within. He is with us and desires to lead and guide us in all truth. (John 16:13) Much as a river brings forth life, the Holy Spirit, if not hindered or blocked, will bring forth the fruit of righteousness. We need to learn how to open the gate so the River of Life can flow through our lives to those who are in our sphere of influence. To God be the Glory, great things He has done!

Chapter 7

WHAT OCCURRED AT THE GATES?

As you read about all of the different gates in the Old Testament and see the symbolism, consider all the ways each gate relates to prayer and intercession. There is a prayer application to be implemented at every gate!

God loves the gates! Let's think about all the things the Lord loves. He loves his children. He loves souls. He loved the world so much that he gave his only begotten son. He loves a cheerful giver. He loves righteousness. What else does he love? He loves the gates. *"His foundation is in the Holy mountains; the LORD loves the gates of Zion more than all the other dwelling places of Jacob."* (Ps. 87:1)

Have you ever seen that in the Bible before? Why would the Lord love gates? I asked the Lord about it, and I want to share some of what he revealed to me. In Psalm 87, the Word declares that the Lord loves the gates of Zion more than all the other dwelling places of Jacob. Jacob had 12 sons and those 12 sons were given an inheritance. They all had land, but God said he loves the gates because they are the places where his people come into his kingdom. The gates allow us to come into his presence. A gate goes two ways— in and out. God reaches out through the gates, through us, to meet the world. We are his gateway to the world. We are his vehicles. We are his instruments. He can come through us to meet other people, just like we go through Yeshua to meet and fellowship with him. People get saved at the gate. That's why he loves the gates of Zion more than any other dwelling place of Jacob. So when he is saying, "Go through, go through the gates," he is speaking to himself and to us!

Let's look at what occurred at the gates.

Wisdom Utters Her Voice

Wisdom utters her voice at the gates. "*Wisdom is too exalted for a fool, He does not open his mouth in the gate.*" (Prov. 24:7) Wisdom is knowledge applied. If we have knowledge and do not apply it, we are foolish. Conversely, when we have knowledge and apply it, we are wise. For example, if I know that I need to bless the Lord at all times (Ps. 34) and I choose not to bless the Lord, then I am not exercising wisdom. "At all times" means even when you have no money, when you are sick, disappointed, disillusioned, angry, frustrated and when you are at the end of yourself. When the Word says, *"Bless the Lord at all times,"* it means just that — no matter what the circumstance, we are to bless the LORD! Let's apply this principle to what is revealed in Proverbs 24:7. Because of this verse we know that wisdom is too exalted for a fool, because he doesn't open his mouth in the gate. By contrast, Wisdom speaks when she sees the enemy at the gate. In the case of Psalm 34, that enemy is anything that would cause us to not want to bless the Lord!

Let's look at Proverbs 1, which states, *"Wisdom shouts in the street, She lifts her voice in the square; at the head of the noisy streets She cries out; at the entrance of the gates in the city, she utters her sayings..."* (Prov. 1:20-21) This whole chapter speaks about wisdom. Wisdom cries out, and at the entrance of the gates of the city she utters her sayings. Who is crying out? Wisdom. Wisdom is crying out. It is wise to raise your voice at the gates.

Courts of Justice

Courts of justice convened at the gates in ancient times. *"You shall appoint for yourselves judges and officers in all of your towns which the LORD your God is giving you according to your tribes, and they shall judge the people with righteous judgment."* (Deut. 16:18) Now the Hebrew word that is translated "towns" in the NASB is actually sha'ar(im) which, as we discussed in chapter 1, means "gates." God is a just God. Our cases can be presented before him and we can trust in his justice. He is in covenant relationship with us, therefore we can come before his court to claim what rightfully belongs to us according to what is written in his Word. He watches over his Word to perform it. He inhabits the praises of his people. He is our salvation, healer and deliverer. He is a very present help in time of trouble. As we enter into his gates with thanksgiving and his courts with praise, he inhabits us. If he inhabits us, then we are healthy. We have more than enough because one of his names is *El Shaddai* — the God that is more than enough. He is *Jehovah Jireh* — the One who sees ahead and makes provision. He is our provider and knows what our needs are going to be. These are just a few of the innumerable promises we can claim in the courtroom of heaven.

Land was Redeemed

Land was redeemed at the gates. We have a detailed description of this kind of transaction in the book of Ruth.

> *Now Boaz went up to the gate and sat down*
> *there, and behold, the close relative of whom*

Boaz spoke was passing by, so he said, "Turn aside, friend, sit down here." And he turned aside and sat down. He took ten men of the elders of the city and said, "Sit down here." So they sat down. Then he said to the closest relative, "Naomi, who has come back from the land of Moab, has to sell the piece of land which belonged to our brother Elimelech. So I thought to inform you, saying, 'Buy it before those who are sitting here, and before the elders of my people. If you will redeem it, redeem it; but if not, tell me that I may know; for there is no one but you to redeem it, and I am after you.'" And he said, "I will redeem it." (Ruth 4:1-4)

We can now apply our understanding of this function of the gate to the Lord's Prayer. *"'Our Father who is in heaven, hallowed be Your name. Your kingdom come. Your will be done, on earth as it is in heaven.'"* (Matt. 6:9-10) What does God mean when He says *"on earth?"* We are made out of dust, or earth. *"Your kingdom come, Your will be done on earth"* — on me — *"as it is in heaven."* Land was redeemed at the gates. You were redeemed at *the* gate, Yeshua Himself. When you accepted him as your Messiah, you were redeemed.

Proclamations and Declarations

Proclamations and declarations were made at the gates.

> *Thus the LORD said to me, 'Go and stand in the public gate, through which the kings of Judah come in and go out as well as all of the gates of Jerusalem; and say to them, "Listen to the word of the Lord, kings of Judah and all Judah, and all inhabitants of Jerusalem who come in through these gates."* (Jer. 17:19-20)

God didn't say, "Go to the church and proclaim my Word." He said, "Go to the public gate, and there, at that gate, proclaim my Word." Newsflash! It is time to get out into the public square and proclaim the Word of the living God!

"*And the master said to the slave, 'Go out into the highways and along the hedges, and compel them to come in, so that my house may be filled.'*"(Luke 14:23) God's Word is truth and when we publicly proclaim it, it goes forth and does not return empty or void, but it accomplishes what it was sent to do. (Isa. 55:11) God's Word is more powerful than a two-edged sword. (Heb. 4:12) People often pray about their problems but they don't pray according to the Word of God. You need to know what the Bible says about your situation. He watches over his Word to perform it. (Jer. 1:12) He doesn't watch over our words to perform them. We are to remind God of his Word. We need to speak or proclaim his Word. It is wonderful to speak in tongues and pray in tongues, especially when we do not know how to pray; but the Word of God and its proclamation is also a critical key. One of the weapons of our warfare is the Word of God and we must proclaim that Word at the gate. You might ask how we do that. The revelation of how to pray at the gates is coming. Just keep reading.

Councils of State

Councils of State were held at the gates.

> *Now the king of Israel and Jehoshaphat the king of Judah were sitting each on his throne, arrayed in their robes, and they were sitting at the threshing floor at the entrance of the gate of Samaria; and all the prophets were prophesying before them.* (2 Chron. 18:9)

The kings of Judah came in and out of the gates. Governmental authorities, Councils of State and Heads of State all met at the gates. God is revealing to go to those that are in charge and go straight to the strongmen. This gate warfare does not merely engage the little subordinate spirits or manifestations of the strongmen. Warfare at the gates confronts the principal strongmen in charge. They have the authority. You want to pray against the stronghold at the gate and not the manifestation. There are 12 strongholds that correspond to the 12 tribes which are named after the 12 sons of Jacob. As we mentioned earlier, the number 12 is significant in the Bible. It represents governmental authority. In the Bible you will see that, in addition to the 12 tribes of Israel, Ishmael had 12 sons who are called the 12 princes, and of course there are the 12 apostles.

Public Commendations

Public commendations were made at the gates. *"Her husband is known in the gates, when he sits among the elders of the land."* (Prov. 31:23) *"Give her the product of her hands and let her works praise her in the gates."* (Prov. 31:31) What do we do when coming into God's presence? We enter his gates with thanksgiving and his courts with praise. What do we do? We commend him.

The Gates were Shut at Nightfall

Think about this; if you are sleeping, demons cannot operate through you. A Spirit of Murder, for example, is obviously unable to operate when a person is sleeping. (One exception to this general principle might be the ability of demons to operate in dreams). Since gates were shut at nightfall, it is wonderful to be able to pray early in the morning because there is less demonic activity going on at that time. Demons need a body to operate through. They are disembodied spirits that need a body to occupy or influence to express their natures.

Gates were a Chief Point of Attack in War

"New gods were chosen; then war was in the gates." (Judg. 5:8) If you were going to attack a city, you would go to the entrance and attack the gate. In the Old Testament, battering rams were used to attack at the gates. *"Into his right hand came the divination, 'Jerusalem', to set battering rams, to open the mouth for slaughter, to lift up the voice with a battle cry, to set battering rams against the gates, to cast up ramps, to build a siege wall."* (Ezek. 21:22)

The above scripture also indicates that battering rams were used against the gates. Let's go back to Isaiah 62:12, which says that the holy people of the Lord are called *"sought out, a city not forsaken."* Since we are being likened to a city, do we have natural enemies coming to us with battering rams? Of course not! Well, wait just a minute. On second thought, these days we have to deal with knife intifada attacks, suicide bombers, armed terrorists, and various kinds of unsaved, deceived emissaries of the Kingdom of Darkness. One has to be strengthened by disciplined prayer, Bible study and strategic intercession just to go out grocery shopping! Don't forget to be thankful that there is still food on those grocery store shelves. In addition, we have an enemy who is battering our minds daily with lies, suspicions, accusations, falsehood and deception. His battering of our thought life is constant.

While living in Jerusalem years ago, I never had a problem with fear, although I don't like snakes. One day I was walking down the street in Jerusalem and a snake slithered down the street right next to me. Did I jump? No, I didn't. You are talking about a person who would jump because I mistook my own finger under a glass of water I was holding for a bug! Yet in Jerusalem, I had no fear.

When I returned to Jacksonville, Florida, I realized that irrational fear was the demonic stronghold over that city. When I came into Jacksonville, I came under that irrational Spirit of Fear and was tormented for months. Irrational fear was influencing me. Irrational fear and torment had me thinking thoughts like, "It's never going to get better ... it's always going to be like this... it's hopeless." The enemy's job is to batter your mind with lies. If your mind is not being bombarded, you are either not recognizing your enemy or you are dead. When we get those suggestions or thoughts, what do we do with them? Do we receive them? Absolutely not. We take those thoughts captive to the obedience of Messiah. (2 Cor. 10:5) The Word of God allows us to pull down those strongholds and fortresses.

It is good to praise the Lord. *"From the rising of the sun to its setting the name of the Lord is to be praised."* (Ps. 113:3) Praise him before the battle and he will ambush your enemies. Praise him during the battle because the joy of the Lord is your strength and he inhabits the praises of his people. (Neh. 8:10, Ps. 22:3) Praise him after the battle for the victory! Then feast!

> *Praise the Lord! Sing to the Lord a new song, And His praise in the Congregation of the godly ones. Let Israel be glad in his Maker; Let the sons of Zion rejoice in their King. Let them praise His name with dancing; Let them sing praises to Him with timbrel and lyre. For the Lord takes pleasure in His people; He will*

beautify the afflicted ones with salvation. Let the godly ones exult in glory; Let them sing for joy on their beds. Let the high praises of God be in their mouth, and a two-edged sword in their hand, to execute vengeance on the nations, and punishment on the peoples, To bind their kings with chains, And their nobles with fetters of iron, To execute on them the judgment written; This is an honor for all His godly ones. Praise the Lord! (Ps. 149)

Why do you think Psalm 149 says, *"Let them sing for joy on their beds?"* Because the joy of the Lord is your strength (Neh. 8:10), so if you have that joy you want to be out of bed! You want to be dancing! You could be doing more than singing. You can't dance in bed. God is just letting you know, "I know you are on your bed. Sing to me and I will give you strength." In the presence of the Lord there is strength, power and might. In the presence of the Lord there is fullness of joy. The joy of the Lord is your strength, so if you are on your bed, sing to him!

When you dance, when you sing, when you twirl and when you "hallel," you are binding the kings or strongmen with chains. (Psalm 149) Through your high praises, you are literally binding up the enemy. It is time that we use the weapons of our warfare, which are mighty through the pulling down of fortresses and strongholds. (2 Cor. 10:4) We need to batter the enemy for a while.

Gates were often Razed or Burned

Once, I was speaking with a friend who was going to be traveling overseas on a mission trip. I started praying for her, and as I did I saw a wall of fire. I asked her if I could pray for this wall of fire to be around her. With her permission I continued to pray. In the spirit I could see this fire above her head and around her. A couple of days after that the Lord showed me a passage in Zechariah where God was speaking about Jerusalem. Zechariah states, *"For I, declares the LORD, will be a wall of fire around her, and I will be the glory in her midst."* (Zech. 2:5) We are the New Jerusalem and God is a wall of fire around us. Because of this, the fiery darts from the enemy can't touch us. We understand this from the principles of fire's behavior in nature. Firefighters will often start a backfire to fight fire with fire. When the fire they want to extinguish touches the back fire, there is nothing left for fuel – nothing left to burn! This is what extinguishes the destructive fire. If you are going to be burned, let it be with God's fire, which is able to cleanse you and purify you. You will come forth as gold! (Job 23:10) Don't allow the fire of the enemy to torment you.

When we enter into intercession we can pray, "God be a wall of fire around me! Let your glory be in my midst. Hide me in the cleft of the rock. (Exod. 33:22) Put me under the shadow of your wings." (Ps. 17:8) Psalm 91 is a Psalm of protection. I recommend that we pray Psalm 91 over ourselves daily — especially in the days we are living in.

> *No evil will befall you, nor will any plague come near your tent. For He will give His angels charge concerning you, to guard you in all of your ways... A thousand may fall at your side, and ten thousand at your right hand; but it shall not approach you... For you have made the LORD my refuge Even the Most High, your dwelling place.* (Ps. 91:11, 7 & 9)

What is our responsibility? It is to dwell in the secret place of the Most High God.

We need to remind God of his Word. As we do that, the angels of the Lord go out and perform his Word. It is important to sow the Word of God in our hearts. David sowed the Word of God in his heart so that he would not sin against God. (Ps. 119:11) We need to know his Word so that when trials come, we will be ready to bless the Lord at all times and have his praise continually in our mouths. (Ps. 34:1)

It is essential that our knowledge of his Word penetrates our hearts and our actions. Intellectual understanding is not enough. Embrace God and his Word with every fiber of your being. Know that you are a gatekeeper in your city, in your family, in your church and in your region. God has entrusted you with great power, authority and responsibility. When you hear this revelation and you implement it, you will participate with the Holy Spirit in effecting change on earth for the Kingdom of God. You will restrain the powers of darkness and make a way for the Lord in the wilderness.

When I first began to comprehend this revelation, I struggled with a lot of fear in my life so I began to go to the Gate of Gad. Gad means "good fortune" and fear happens to attack at the Gate of Gad. The manifestations of fear are anxiety, stress and worry. One day, while watching a commercial on television, I noticed that the name Gad is also the acronym for General Anxiety Disorder (G.A.D.) People who suffer with that anxiety disorder take a medication called Paxil to cope with the fear and anxiety. Instead they could simply bind fear at the Gate of Gad and fill their minds with the Word of God. Fear not! When I was tormented with fear, I would go to the Gate of Gad and bind fear and begin to declare God's Word. My declaration would be,

"The Lord is my light and my salvation; Whom shall I fear? The Lord is the defense of my life; Whom shall I dread? When evildoers came upon me to devour my flesh, my adversaries and my enemies, they stumbled and fell. Though a host encamp against me, my heart will not fear; Though war arise against me, In spite of this I shall be confident." (Ps. 27:1-3)

What was I doing? Renewing my mind. What else was I doing? Releasing angels to go out and perform the Word of God. The enemy at the Gate of Gad is trying to batter my mind and get me into all the dread, fear, poverty and everything else that comes with that. God watches over his Word to perform it. How does he do that? Psalm 103:20 says that the angels obey the voice of God's Word. I encourage you to put voice to God's Word through declarations and proclamations!

Acts of Idolatry

Acts of idolatry occurred at the gates. *"The priest of Zeus, whose temple was just outside of the city, brought oxen and garlands to the gates, and wanted to offer sacrifice with the crowds."* (Acts 14:13) I had an experience in which I was confronted with idolatry at the gate of a city and I want to share with you how to handle this knowledge wisely. I was on the internet and found something intriguing on a site that the Lord had given me permission to go into. I'm not going to reveal the site, but it talked about the city of Atlanta, Georgia. Atlanta is nicknamed "a gated city." The website gave all of the information about a particular "sect" that is very organized and well known throughout the world. I wouldn't call this group a cult, but it is a non-Christian, ungodly group that gathers together and is in deception. The Lord led me to read the acceptance speech of the high priest in this particular group in which he gave all of the history of the organization. He described their history in England referring to a deed and a warrant. The speech gave dates and details pertinent to the organization. I started to realize that the Lord was releasing much understanding. When the Lord releases information to us, we have to know what to do with that knowledge. If you are an intercessor and God gives you information, you may often feel you have to run to someone else with the information. I've done that myself. We run to the Pastor. We start running right away and want to do something with that information! We really need to wait on the Lord for his counsel, which is a sign of maturity.

When the Lord was revealing things to me on this website, the first thing that came to my mind was that I needed to get this to an apostle in the Atlanta area. God has given each of us a measure of authority. All of us have been given authority within our families. Additionally, some have been given a local call and authority over a city. Still others, have been given an international call. It is critical to know where and what your boundaries are, because that is the only place you have God's authority and his protection. At that time, I had a sense that God had given me a boundary of authority so that I could go anywhere in the southeastern part of the USA as far north as Washington, DC and as far west as Dallas/ Ft. Worth. Atlanta fell within that area. I could have taken the authority and gone to that gate in Atlanta and prayed, however I did not sense the prompting of the Lord to do that. I felt that I needed to share that information with a spiritual authority in the area. When the Spirit of the Lord entrusts you with something, have the maturity to seek him and find out what he wants you to do with it.

Timing is so critical when dealing with the things of God. Once, God gave me a word for a church that I was attending. It was a powerful word, however it was delivered prematurely and was not received. Hearts had not been prepared to receive the word. We can speak things that are true, but if the people are not ready to receive it, then what good is it? You want to give a word in due season. You want to go according to God's timing. It is not good to get ahead of

God. Be sensitive. Know what God is saying and what He expects you to do with what He has given you. Remember... he leads; we follow.

Experienced Officers stationed at the Gates

Experienced officers are stationed at the gates. The enemy is organized with ranks, just as the military has ranks and levels of authority. Just as the military requires submission to those in authority of a higher rank and file, the enemy's kingdom works the same way. Not only does the enemy have experienced officers but he also has an attack strategy. The devil is smart. He is not going to offer me crack cocaine because I don't have a problem with crack. He might offer me an M&M or a piece of pumpkin pie because those will create more of a problem for me than crack or alcohol. The devil is smart enough to know my weaknesses. So what are your weaknesses? I've got news for you — the devil knows! He knows your weaknesses. He knows how to push your buttons so he can set you up. Much of the time you will fall for it until you recognize the enemy and say, "No way devil! Get behind me Satan!" The devil really isn't that creative. He will use the same trap every time. Whatever your weaknesses are, remember, there are experienced officers at the gates waiting for just the right time to tempt you so that you may fall.

Manifestations of a demonic stronghold may be in operation. If you pray against that manifestation you can cast it out, but if you don't attack the stronghold, the demon that was giving you the manifestation can come right back under his higher authority.

The first time I taught this was on October 31st of 1999. There was a certain couple in that meeting that caught hold of this very truth – the enemy's rank. They took the logos word (instructional word) and it became a rhema word (active word) to them. Unbeknownst to me, they had a prison ministry. Through their ministry, the captives were being set free because they had received the revelation of confronting the strongman and not the lesser demons that were manifesting.

One morning, I had an experience that demonstrated this principle. I was really restless and I couldn't understand why. I could take authority over a spirit of restlessness if I wanted to, and cast it out, but I sensed that there was something more to what was happening. I decided to call a friend and ask her to pray with me. As soon as I was finished talking to her, I felt prompted to search through my study notes to see what the manifestations of restlessness were. Restlessness manifests at the Gate of Naphtali, but the demonic stronghold that attacks at that gate is jealousy! (I'll explain this more in depth in the following chapters as you read on). Now, I didn't feel jealous at all. I felt restless. Nonetheless, I bound and took authority over the spirit of jealousy and the restlessness left. Sometimes action comes before understanding. We often quote the scriptures, stating that the fervent, effectual prayer of a righteous man availeth much. (James 5:16) We can be righteous in the eyes of God. We can be very fervent in our prayers, but if we're not effectual it's not going to avail much. We're going to talk about those 12 demonic strongholds and the manifestations as we continue. I believe it will completely enhance and intensify the way you pray!

If you've ever read the book, *God's Dream Team* by Tommy Tenney, he makes reference to what he calls "gate keepers." The following is paraphrased from Tommy Tenney's book:

> This term, gatekeepers, can refer to pastors, intercessors, and virtually anyone who exercises spiritual influence. Even in the secular realm, there are certain professionals, politicians, and influential people whose authority is channeled in and out of a city. Influence is channeled in and out of a city through these gatekeepers. In God's kingdom, you have been

assigned as a gatekeeper. As you seek God and meditate in His Word, you will develop into an experienced officer in the army of the Lord. You have power and authority. If we intend to see the spiritual atmosphere of our city change, we must be willing to be spiritual gatekeepers. (Tenney 1999)

Tommy Tenney writes about Jerusalem being a type of a church.

This great city had 12 gates, and each gate had a name. Which gate is yours? Do you know where your place is? Do you know who and where the other gatekeepers are? Who will stand united in the gates for the city? (Tenney 1999)

Remember, the New Jerusalem has 12 gates. The number 12 represents governmental authority. To make this point clearer, let me quote Tommy Tenney from his book, *God's Dream Team*. *"So what good does it do if you guard your gate, but I don't guard mine? The city will still be vulnerable because of a lack of unity. If you lock your gate but I refuse to lock mine then there's at least one major entrance into the city that's accessible to the enemy."* (Tenney 1999)

You are a spiritual gatekeeper in your geographical area. You have the ability, power and authority to allow or forbid (bind or loose) influence in and out of your city. You don't want perversion in your city. You don't want familiar spirits in your city. FORBID THEM! You need to be in prayer asking God, "What are the strongholds over this area? Who are the experienced officers that the enemy has placed at the gates?" It's amazing what God will reveal. As we begin to do this, revival is going to break out. God has not forgotten you. Timing and trust are two keys in all of this teaching that I am sharing with you. God's plan for you has to do with the end time revival. It has to do with timing. Trust him. Timing is so important. There is no question that we are living in the end times. This teaching and the revelation that God has given is an end time teaching. If you take hold of this teaching, it will usher in his glory and his presence in your area of the world or wherever you may be. God calls us to hear his voice and obey, no matter what the cost. Are you willing to obey no matter what the cost? It might cost you a lot. God has said, "I will be your shelter, and I'm causing you to die daily." That's the key. Not my will, God, but yours be done. We need to be asking God how to go through the gates, and be willing to obey no matter what he tells us.

We need to understand that we are gatekeepers and we can enter through his gates. We enter his gates with thanksgiving and his courts with praise. In order to do that effectively, we have to know who we are. Once my mentor said to me that God was being very quiet about what he was going to do because of three things that he wants us to do, first:

1. He wants us to know who we are in him.
2. He wants us to flow.
3. He wants us to grow.

He wants us to know who we are in him. he wants us to grow in what he's already shown us and then to flow in it. He wants to mature us in the Spirit.

> *And He gave some as apostles, and some as prophets, and some as evangelists, and some as pastors and teachers, for the equipping of the saints for the work of service, to the building up of the body of Christ; until we all attain to the unity of the faith, and of the knowledge of the Son of God, to a mature man, to the measure of the stature which belongs to the fullness of Christ. (Eph. 4:11-13)*

Some of us have not been doing what we know to do. One of those things is to enter his gates with thanksgiving and his courts with praise. *"But you are a chosen race, a royal priesthood, a holy nation, a people for God's own possession, so that you may proclaim the excellencies of Him who has called you out of darkness into His marvelous light."* (1 Pet. 2:9) Proclaiming his excellencies brings you into his presence. You're a royal priesthood. You are a holy nation. You're a peculiar people who have been called out of darkness by God. You're special! He has chosen you. You have to know that inside.

As I mentioned in chapter 2, I had been an intercessor for a number of years when the Lord began to teach me about Isaiah 62:10-11. Let's take another look at it: *"Go through, go through the gates, clear the way for the people, build up, build up a highway, remove the stones. Say to the daughter of Zion, Lo your salvation comes."* I knew that it had something to do with intercession but the full revelation took time to unfold. If I say to you, "Go through the gates," but you don't really understand what that means, what are you going to do? Action comes after understanding. When God says to us, "Go through, go through the gates," many times we're just standing there because we don't know what to do. As we continue in the passage we read, *"Clear the way for the peoples."* What does this mean? Clear the way for the people. Build up a highway. Remove the stones. As you read on, I want to shed some light, specifically, on what these things mean. If you understand them, then you can implement the prayer strategy in this teaching. You can become an authority in them. God can give you keys that can open doors, keys to give freedom. Think about somebody in jail. If you give them keys, they can go free. If they've got the keys and they don't do anything with them, they stay in jail. But if you give them the keys and they unlock the doors, they're out! So I can give you keys and I can give you understanding, but if you don't use the keys, you stay in jail and the captives stay in jail in your city. If you grab hold of this understanding and you grab hold of this teaching and you implement it, then we all go free. Glory to God!

Chapter 8

THE CITY OF GOD

"Great is the Lord and, greatly to be praised, in the city of our God, His holy mountain." (Ps. 48:1)

"And He carried me away in the Spirit to a great and high mountain, and showed me the holy city, Jerusalem, coming down out of heaven from God having the glory of God. Her brilliance was like a very costly stone, as a stone of crystal-clear jasper. It had a great and high wall with twelve gates, and at the gates were twelve angels, and names were written on them, which are those of the twelve tribes of the sons of Israel." (Rev. 21:10-12)

can remember back to a time in my life when I felt so defeated that all I did was lay in bed. I had no victory in my life. One day, I think God looked at me and understood that I was "dead." By that, I mean that he could see that I had come to the end of myself, and I understood that I couldn't do anything in my own strength. I needed him. When I was ready to get myself out of the way, he was ready to move. I was waiting on God, but in reality, God was waiting on me. He was waiting for me to die. At the appointed time, he gave me a vision. The vision was the New Jerusalem coming down out of heaven. I heard a voice saying, "Nancy! Go through the gates!" At that time, I had been an intercessor for a number of years. I knew that this scripture from Isaiah 62 had to do with intercession, but I didn't yet have the revelation of its significance. God was saying, "Go through the gates!" The picture that he gave me was the New Jerusalem coming down out of heaven, but I saw spiritual strongholds that would not allow me to get through the gates. I read the scripture above from the book of Revelation about the 12 gates, the 12 tribes and the names of the gates being the 12 tribes of the sons of Israel. I saw the angels stationed at the gates, and I saw the New Jerusalem but I couldn't go through the gates.

Prompted by what the Lord showed me, I began to research what the meanings of the tribes and their names were, because God was saying, "Go through, go through the gates." Here is what I discovered...

Reuben means "behold the son".
Simeon means "hearing."
Judah means "let God be praised."
Zebulon means "dwelling."
Asher means "happy."
Gad means "good fortune."
Naphtali means "my wrestling."
Dan means "judge."
Issachar means "man of hire."
Benjamin means "son of my right hand."
Joseph means "one who increases."
Levi means "joined" or "joint heir."

I looked at these names and the Holy Spirit quickened me to get the stronghold teaching that I had heard at Orlando Christian Center. I had sat under the teaching of Pastor Benny Hinn for a number of years. What the Holy Spirit was referring to was a teaching on strongholds that I had written in my Bible. When I looked at my notes from Pastor Benny Hinn's teaching, I saw that there were 12 strongholds. Remember when Yeshua divided the fish and the bread? How many baskets were left after he fed five thousand?

Twelve. Why 12? Twelve is the number of governmental authority. The Holy Spirit was showing me the connection between the strongholds that Pastor Hinn taught and the meaning of the names of the 12 tribes. Did they correlate? Yes, they did! Each stronghold from those teaching notes matched up to one of the tribes of Israel. Let me show you how they correlated.

Reuben means "behold the son." One of the strongholds is the Anti-Messiah (or Anti-Christ) Spirit. "Anti" means against, so Anti-Messiah is against the Messiah or Anointed one. What does the Anti-Messiah Spirit (or we could say Anti-Anointed One Spirit) want you to do? It wants to prevent you from beholding the Son of God; not to behold the Messiah; not to have a saving relationship with Yeshua. That is what the Anti-Messiah Spirit does; it separates you from Messiah.

I received further revelation on this spirit during a week I spent in Thomaston, Georgia, at Pleasant Valley Church. Dr. Henry Wright, who is the pastor at that church, wrote a book called *A More Excellent Way*. I would highly recommend that you read it. His ministry also teaches on the Anti-Messiah Spirit, however they call it an Unloving Spirit, which makes perfect sense. The most basic and essential instruction that we receive from both the Old Testament and the New Testament is to love the Lord your God with all your heart, soul, and might; and to love your neighbor as yourself. God is LOVE. The Anti-Messiah Spirit is anti-love. This spirit doesn't want you to love God, love yourself, or love others. It is working to prevent you from receiving and giving God's love, to keep you from loving and accepting yourself, and from loving others.

Simeon means "hearing." What is the stronghold that would attack at that gate? The Deaf and Mute Spirit. This spirit wants to keep you deaf to the things of God.

Judah means "let God be praised." The stronghold that would fight against that gate is perversion which produces hatred towards God.

Zebulon means "dwelling." We are a dwelling place for the Holy Spirit. We are his temple. God wants to dwell with us. He wants to sup with us. He wants to commune with us. We are designed to be his habitation. What stronghold would try and attack at that gate? Familiar Spirits. Familiar Spirits also need a habitation to be able to pass through the generations. They want to usurp what belongs to God. They attack at the Gate of Zebulon.

Asher means "happy." What stronghold would want to attack at that gate? A Spirit of Heaviness.

As I saw these things lining up, I realized that I was receiving revelation. The gates lined up with the strongholds. A light bulb went on in my mind as I realized why

God was saying to me, "Go through, go through the gates." Since going through the gates would put me in his presence, these strongholds were fighting to keep me out.

Gad means "good fortune." *"For I know the plans that I have for you, declares the LORD, plans for welfare and not for calamity to give you a future and a hope."* (Jer. 29:11) God's plans are good plans for us. What tries to attack at the Gate of Gad? A Spirit of Fear. Fear gives us negative thinking filled with doubt, unbelief and dread.

Naphtali means "my wrestling." Jealousy attacks at this gate. We do not wrestle against flesh and blood but against spiritual principalities and wicked powers in high places (Eph. 6:12). We are not to wrestle horizontally with people, but are to wrestle vertically with the spirits who are controlling the people. The enemy tries to get us into wrestling with each other through competition, jealousy, strife and division to stop us from wrestling with the powers of darkness.

Dan means "judge." What stronghold would attack at that gate? A Spirit of Bondage. A judge will either set you free or lock you up. Yeshua didn't come into the world to condemn it. He came into the world to save it (John 3:17). Bondage tries to keep you bound instead of giving you freedom. Where the Spirit of the Lord is, there is liberty. God wants to liberate us. Yeshua came to mend the broken hearted and set the captives free (Luke 4:18).

Issachar means "man of hire." When you hire a man, he becomes your servant. The enemy wants us to serve him. How does Satan get people to serve him? Through a Spirit of Whoredom, which manifests itself through the love of money and the love of the world. These are the ways that Satan says, "Serve me. Don't serve God!" The Bible explains that we are to love the Lord with all our heart, all of our strength, and our entire mind. The enemy tries to get us to serve and love the things of the world. The Bible plainly explains that if we love the world and the things of this world, that the love of the Father isn't in us (1 John 2:15).

Benjamin means "son of my right hand." Yeshua humbled himself and he was exalted to the right hand of the Father. What enemy would attack at this gate? A Spirit of Pride. Pride is in direct opposition to humility.

Joseph means "one who increases or gathers." When you increase, you think about increasing in strength, effectiveness in the kingdom, or even in finances. God is always thinking about increase and multiplication. What does the enemy try to do? Rob you. He does this through a Spirit of Infirmity. Picture a healthy plant. It is fruitful and it reproduces. Now envision a sick plant. It dies. Infirmity is a robber. Infirmity is designed to make you decrease and diminish until it kills you.

Levi means "joined" or "joint heir." We need to know who we are in Messiah. We are joined together with Yeshua. We are heirs to the kingdom of God. A Lying Spirit attacks at the Gate of Levi trying to convince us that we are not who the Word of God says we are.

There are 12 gates representing the 12 tribes of the sons of Israel. There are also 12 strongholds stationed at the gates. There are also angels at the gates. All of this came together as the Holy Spirit was showing me a vision of the New Jerusalem. At that time, I came before the Lord and acknowledged what he was showing me, however I asked him for a scriptural reference. I told the Lord, "I need something to back this up, (that is that there were 12 strongholds at the gates as well) because I don't want to go outside of the Word." I didn't want to teach heresy and God knew that. We need to know that what we believe God is showing us is not just our imagination. In order to do that, we need to base everything on what his Word says. I asked the Lord to give me a reference to show that these strongholds are also at the gates. He answered my prayer and took me to Ezekiel 8:5. *"Then He said to me, "Son of man, raise your eyes now toward the north." So I raised my eyes toward the north, and behold, to the north of the altar gate was this idol of jealousy at the entrance."* (Ezek. 8:5) This confirmed what the Lord had shown me. Angels are stationed at the gates and strongholds are also stationed at the gates. God was saying, "Go through, go through the gates. Clear the way for the peoples. Build up, build up a highway, remove the stones."

You also need to keep in mind that strongholds are there at the gates and they have to be dealt with. In Psalm 127:5 we are encouraged to speak to the enemy at the gate. *"Like arrows in the hand of a warrior, So are the children of one's youth. How blessed is the man whose quiver is full of them; They shall not be ashamed, When they speak with their enemies in the gate."*

Earlier, we looked at the scripture that tells us that wisdom utters her voice at the gates. (Prov. 1:21) We must speak to the enemy at the gates. Now, don't speak just anything… speak wisdom from God's Word. This is because the angels are watching over God's Word to perform it, or act it out, in response to our prayers and declarations. (Jer. 1:12) Our words will activate the angels to arrest (so to speak) the strongholds who are keeping us out of God's presence. Once that happens, we enter in through the gates. If we speak our words instead of God's Word, or if we complain or murmur, then the angels just stand there! They are actually waiting for us to come into agreement with the Word of God. Once we do, they are able to assist us. The angels are ministering spirits for the heirs of salvation. I encourage you to keep your angels busy by declaring and proclaiming the Word of

God. After all, according to God's Word, they watch over his word to perform it. *Are they not all ministering spirits, sent out to render service for the sake of those who will inherit salvation?* (Heb. 1:14)

We are the gatekeepers in our cities. How do we guard our cities? We speak to the enemy at the gate. You have been given the authority and the angels are waiting for you to exercise that authority so they can perform their duties. *"Then the Lord said to me, You have seen well, for I am watching over My word to perform it."* (Jer. 1:12) *"Bless the LORD, you His angels, Mighty in strength, who perform His word, Obeying the voice of His word!"* (Ps. 103:20) As we declare his Word, the angels obey the voice of his Word. You put voice to his Word!

Chapter 9

EXAMPLE OF PRAYING AT THE GATES

As you have read through this book, you may have a new awareness of areas where you may personally need deliverance. This is a strategy of spiritual warfare that can be implemented for individuals, cities or geographical areas. Here are some practical suggestions for applying this revelation.

This principle is found in Matthew 7:3 where Yeshua tells us to take the logs out of our own eyes before taking the speck out of our brother's. When taking authority over a stronghold, it's important to make sure that none of the manifestations of that stronghold are operating in your life. If you do have manifestations of that stronghold, you must come out of agreement with it.

Here is an example of praying at a gate. Liberty Savaard, the author of *Shattering your Strongholds* calls the sample prayers for spiritual warfare in her books "training wheel prayers." She writes, "Remember what training wheels are for? To help you get balance and forward motion established until you learn a new way of doing something such as learning to ride a bike. *[Sic]* Once you don't need the training wheels anymore, you move out on your own." (Savard 1993) That is also a great metaphor for what I am offering you here. This example is a model for a prayer at the **Gate of Reuben** just to get you started:

Gate Meaning: Behold the Son

Attacking Stronghold: Anti-Messiah

Redemptive Key: The Blood of Yeshua

You would first come into his presence with thanksgiving and into his courts with praise for "Beholding the Son:"

> *Father, you are my God and you are my King. I bless you today and I thank you that you have revealed yourself to me. I have nothing to offer you this day but my praise and my love for you. I know that apart from you I can do nothing, so I ask you to fill me with your presence today, Lord.*

Apply the redemptive key, in this case, the blood of Yeshua:

As I come before you, I apply the blood of Yeshua to my family, my future, my finances and myself. Through the blood of Yeshua you have made my sins that were scarlet, as white as snow. I thank you that you have taken off my filthy rags and clothed me with robes of righteousness.

Speak to the enemy at the gate, in this case, Anti-Messiah Spirit:

You told me that it is wise to speak to the enemy at the gate, so I come before the Gate of Reuben and I bind an Anti-Messiah Spirit from operating in my life, my family's lives, my congregation, our public schools or in our government.

Make your requests to the Lord in the realm of beholding the Son:

Holy Spirit, help me to behold the Son of righteousness today. The Word says that as I behold him, I will become like him. Cause me to walk in your ways and be obedient to your commandments. I don't want "religious" activity today Lord, I want you! It is not by power, nor by might, but by your Spirit — Your yoke is easy and light. Teach me your ways Lord — lead and guide me. Father, if I have acted legalistically in any way, open my eyes. Lead me in liberty and freedom. You said, "Where the Spirit of the Lord is, there is liberty." I desire to worship you alone. Thank you for the blood of Messiah. Thank you for cleansing me and making me acceptable through your Son, Yeshua. Help me to accept my weaknesses, that I may also accept your grace and extend it to those who do not know you. Lord I want to lift up the Jewish people and all people who do not yet acknowledge you as Messiah.

As you make specific requests, it may be appropriate to address the enemy at the gate further:

I speak to the Anti-Messiah Spirit, and bind you according to God's word. The blood of Yeshua is against you, Anti-Messiah Spirit.

Continue making requests of the Lord (and addressing the enemy at the gate) as led by the Holy Spirit:

Father, I come before you at the Gate of Reuben and I decree and declare that, "All of Israel will be saved." I come into agreement with you when you said, "I will be your God, and you shall be my people. Because you are precious in my sight, I will give other men in exchange for your life." Lord, you came for the lost sheep of the house of Israel. Reveal yourself to your people for your Name's sake. Do not forget your covenant to bless those who bless Israel and curse those who curse Israel. I speak blessings to Israel in Yeshua's Name, Amen.

You can use this example as a template for prayers at any of the gates, simply substituting the meaning of the gate, the corresponding stronghold and redemptive key. In addition, the Holy Spirit may lead you to sing a song, dance or declare a particular scripture at a gate. As you begin to pray along these lines, I believe the Holy Spirit will begin to give you insight and wisdom on how to pray strategically and effectively in any situation — and start to exercise a new level of authority as a child of the Most High God.

If you are interested in reading sample prayers for the other gates, you can find them in my previous book,

Weapons of Mass Deliverance. As you rely on the Holy Spirit, he is faithful to lead you and pray through you at every gate.

My experience with three-year-old David[1*] demonstrates an extraordinary move of God I witnessed after I discerned an enemy stronghold at the Gate of Reuben operating against him. I was asked to share the revelation on the gates at a home group in the Atlanta area a number of years ago. After the meeting, David's grandmother asked me what was wrong with him. You see, he exhibited behavior consistent with a mild form of autism. I asked the Lord what was wrong with David and got the impression that the young boy was oppressed with an Anti-Messiah spirit. I asked the mother, father and the grandmother to pray with me as I led them in a prayer of repentance for this spirit in their generations on both sides, all the way back to Adam. Then I took authority over the Anti-Messiah Spirit and prayed a deliverance prayer, although the child was not even in the room. After we prayed, we went back into the other room and, before our eyes, witnessed a dramatic change in this young boy. We were all stunned. When the neighbor who lived across the street came over the next morning, his behavior was so noticeably different she asked, "What happened to little David?"

---

[1] * Not his real name

I warned the mom that since he was only three, the spirit would probably try to return. She would have to exercise her authority and not allow it. This is exactly what happened, but she exercised her authority, the enemy was defeated and the little one was totally delivered.

Just a few years ago, I attended his Bar Mitzvah. He did a beautiful job and blessed all of us with his wit and charm. As I enjoyed his great sense of humor, I just sat there crying, thinking how good God is! To God be the glory, great things he has done!

Chapter 10

SHOUT IT OUT!

Sometimes in scripture you will notice that portions of scripture are repeated two or three times. "Go through, go through the gates" is one example. We learn through repetition. If we don't get it the first time around, we come around the bend again until we do. You now understand:

1) It is wise to speak to the enemy at the gate;
2) Which stronghold attacks at which gate;
3) You are to go through the gates into the presence of God;
4) There are redemptive keys which are to be released at the particular gate.

Those keys are listed in Appendix B. Now it is time to illuminate the power behind praying at the gates!

Scripture tells us that the natural comes before the spiritual. (1 Cor. 15:46) With this principle in mind, let's take a look at the natural first regarding proclaiming and declaring the Word of God and see how it is applied in the spirit.

The Significance of Shechem

You'd never know it today, but Shechem, the site of modern day Nablus, provided the most important crossroads in central Israel. Because of its central location as a vital intersection, Shechem often found itself in major events in the biblical narrative. Abraham came first to Shechem when he entered Canaan (Genesis 12:6), and God confirmed the promise to give the land to him there. Later Jacob would return here with his family and settle.

Mounts Gerizim and Ebal

Shechem is located between Mt. Gerizim and Mt. Ebal. It has a rich biblical history beginning with being the place where God promised the land to Abraham, as mentioned above.

You may wonder why I repeated this twice. Primarily because the rights to this land are being contested over and over again. Lies are being repeated and it is past time for the truth to be shouted by the gatekeepers over and over!

After the Exodus, the Lord commanded Israel to go to Shechem and recite the blessings and the curses of the Mosaic Law. (Deut. 27:4) Joshua did this by dividing the nation. *"...Half of them stood in front of Mount Gerizim and half of them in front of Mount Ebal..."* (Josh. 8:33) Shechem stood in the valley between.

Can you envision the nation of Israel shouting the blessings and the curses? In an article for the bibleplaces.com blog, Todd Bolen cites an acoustic experiment conducted in 1879 that demonstrated how the valley would have acted as a natural amphitheater —amplifying the voices of the Hebrew nation as they proclaimed the blessings and curses. (Bolen 2008) Let me say that again. The valley would have acted as a natural amphitheater—amplifying the voices of the Hebrew nation.

We are not standing on either Mount Gerizim or Mount Ebal anymore when we declare and proclaim the Word of God. Remember my story about the Lord asking where I was until I answered, "I am seated with Christ in heavenly places?" Not long after that, I returned to Jacksonville, Florida and was praying at the gates. The Lord asked me another question. He asked if I wanted to know the power behind praying at the gates. You see, I had been teaching this revelation for seven years to prophetic intercessors, pastors and ministry leaders and had done conferences, seminars and workshops, yet I myself did not understand the power behind praying at the gates!

The Lord showed me that now when we declare and proclaim his Word, we are in the courtroom of heaven coming into agreement with the elders in the throne room! It is commonly accepted that 12 of the 24 elders in the throne room of God are the Patriarchs, the sons of Jacob who the gates are named after and 12 of the elders are the Apostles of Yeshua.

Think about this: as you come into agreement with them and declare the Word of God, it is as if your prayers are being amplified! *A cord of three strands is not quickly torn apart.* (Eccles. 4:12) When you are praying at the gates, you are entering the throne room of God. When you declare the will of heaven at a gate, God showed me that it's as if you are reaching your hand back through eternity past and taking hold of the hand of the Patriarch at that gate (such as Benjamin) and taking hold of the hand of one of the Apostles (such as Paul, also a Benjamite) and forming a three-fold cord that cannot be easily broken. You are closing a circuit between heaven and earth which causes the Word of God, which you have declared at the gate, to manifest in the earthly realm. That is the power of praying at the gates!

I was sharing this revelation about the three-fold cord in Savannah, Georgia at a seminar I was doing. At the break, a man approached and asked, "Do you know how many prongs are in a transistor?"

Not being a techie, I replied, "No."

"There are 3. Do you know why?" he continued. Of course I didn't! "For amplification!" he explained.

As you pray at the gates, you come into agreement with the elders in the throne room forming a three-fold cord. This example confirms that your prayers are being amplified. What occurred in the natural at Mount Ebal and Mount Gerazim with the amplification is a picture of how your prayer is amplified when you pray at the gates.

When you pray at the gates you are here:

> *But you have come to Mount Zion and to the city of the living God, the heavenly Jerusalem, and to myriads of angels, to the general assembly and church of the firstborn who are enrolled in heaven, and to God, the Judge of all, and to the spirits of the righteous made perfect, and to Jesus, the mediator of a new covenant, and to the sprinkled blood, which speaks better than the blood of Abel.* (Heb. 12:22-24)

After the Lord showed me the power behind praying at the gates, I found out that there was more to be revealed.

Sometime later I was sharing this with a very small group of women. After I had spoken, I laid my hands on them individually and asked the Lord to give them the revelation I had and even more revelation than he had given me. He answered that prayer quickly! The next day one of the women, who was a prophet, called me to share what the Lord had shown her. She stated that there are many manners of praying including prayers of repentance, supplication, thanksgiving, intercession, petition and agreement. What she was shown is that praying at the gates is the manner of prayer that finally breaks down the wall of partition between Jew and Gentile. For you see, we read that in the New Jerusalem the foundation stones of the walls of the city have the names of the 12 Apostles from the New Testament, which opened the way of salvation to the gentiles, (though the Apostles themselves were Jewish) and the 12 gates have the names of the sons of Jacob from the Old Testament, which established God's covenant with the Israelites. When you come into agreement with them both, what results? Voila! One new man! (Eph. 2:15) Neither Jew nor gentile! (Gal. 3:28) One in Messiah! That is the power behind praying at the gates!

Chapter 11

SPECIAL END NOTE FOR SEASONED INTERCESSORS

For those intercessors that have an interest in spiritual mapping, I have found an interesting connection between this teaching on the Gates and spiritual mapping. I first made the discovery when I was driving through my hometown, Jacksonville, Florida. While driving around I-295, I realized that as I drove in different parts of the perimeter of the city, the way I was praying in tongues would change. One day, as I was on my way to a Pastor's home, I missed the exit and found myself driving from the west side of the city to the east side. I felt the spiritual climate change so significantly that I asked the Lord, "What was that?" I could feel that I was under spiritual oppression and heaviness, especially when I was driving through the west side of the city. The Spirit of the Lord began to show me what was happening in those areas by leading me to Ezekiel 48:

> *These are the exits of the city: on the north side, 4,500 cubits by measurement, shall be the gates of the city, named for the tribes of Israel, three gates toward the north: the gate of Reuben, one; the gate of Judah, one; the gate of Levi, one. On the east side, 4,500 cubits, shall be three gates: the gate of Joseph, one; the gate of Benjamin, one; the gate of Dan, one. On the south side, 4,500 cubits by measurement, shall be three gates: the gate of Simeon, one; the gate of Issachar, one; the gate of Zebulun, one. On the west side, 4,500 cubits, shall be three gates: the gate of Gad, one; the gate of Asher, one; the gate of Naphtali, one. The city shall be 18,000 cubits round about; and the name of the city from that day shall be, "The LORD is there." (Ezek. 48:30-35)*

Using this pattern from Ezekiel, I began to take a look at the spiritual climate of my city, Jacksonville, Florida. Keep in mind the attacking strongholds at each gate listed in chapter 10 to get the clearest picture of the information given to us here in the book of Ezekiel.

The North Gates are Reuben, Judah and Levi.

The strongholds that attack from the North are Anti-Messiah Spirit (Reuben), Spirit of Perversion (Judah), and Lying Spirit (Levi).

The East Gates are Joseph, Benjamin, and Dan.

The strongholds that attack from the East are Spirit of Infirmity (Joseph), Spirit of Pride (Benjamin), and Spirit of Bondage (Dan).

The South Gates are Simeon, Issachar, and Zebulon.

The strongholds that attack from the South are Deaf & Mute Spirit (Simeon), Spirit of Whoredom (Issachar), Familiar Spirits (Zebulon).

The West Gates are Gad, Asher, and Naphtali.

The strongholds that attack from the West are Spirit of Fear (Gad), Spirit of Heaviness (Asher), and Spirit of Jealousy (Naphtali).

When I placed this pattern over my own home city, I found that the manifestations of these strongholds, in fact, often appeared in the neighborhoods and sections of the city that geographically corresponded with the information revealed in Ezekiel chapter 48.

In March of 2003, I was in Israel and was asked to share the Gates teaching with the staff of Emmaus Way Ministries in Tel Aviv. I just gave them a quick overview of the teaching and the staff members wanted to know where the strongholds were located in their city, what the redemptive keys were, as well as the location of the gates. As I began to relate this information to them, they took out a map of the city of Tel Aviv and were amazed at how the manifestations of the strongholds were predominant in the locations of the city corresponding with the text from Ezekiel 48. This is not to say that the manifestations only occur in those locations, but it became apparent that there was a prevalent matching of areas and strongholds that was more than coincidental. This information afforded them the foreknowledge to send teams of intercessors to the areas to specifically target those strongholds. Glory to God.

If you apply this same strategy to your city or area of the country, you may also find some clues to pray effectively through the gates for your region. The one city for which it did not seem to coincide was Washington D.C. In fact, the correlation almost seemed backwards. This actually was no surprise since the city was laid out in a pattern established by the Freemasons. I would love to hear from those of you who further investigate this intercessory key. If you feel prompted to share your discoveries, you can email me at **gatesofprayer12@gmail.com** . May the Lord bless and keep you!

Chapter 12

ENTERING THROUGH THE NARROW GATE

The first time the word "gate" appears in the Bible is in Genesis. That is no surprise since Genesis in Hebrew means "in the beginning." *Now the two angels came to Sodom in the evening as Lot was sitting in the gate of Sodom.* (Gen. 19:1) Here we see two angels at the gate. In this passage, this is a natural gate and both of these angels were servants of the Lord, but let's turn our focus to the gates that are in your mind. There are also two angels at those gates: a servant of the Lord and a fallen angel. Which angel are you going to activate? Are you going to come into agreement with God or the devil? Your destiny is your choice. God gives us free will. If you do not know God in a personal way, you have a choice and are invited to come to him and enter into his Kingdom. If you have already chosen him and know him, the quality of your life depends upon your moment-to-moment choices while serving him. You can accept or reject his precepts, statutes, teachings and instructions. One choice leads to life, one to death. You choose. He wants us to choose life. *"I call heaven and earth to witness against you today, that I have set before you life and death, the blessing and the curse. So choose life in order that you may live, you and your descendants..."* (Deut. 30:19)

Whether you are a Jew or a Gentile, you may find yourself wondering, "Just what does it mean to be born again?" *"And now, if you diligently obey my voice, and shall guard my covenant, then you shall be my treasured possessions above all the peoples; for all the earth is mine."* (Exod. 19:5) This word wasn't given just to Judah but to the whole house of Israel. When the Jews left Egypt, a mixed multitude of people came out among them. Those who were not born Israelites became one with them by joining themselves to the Israelites and accepting the covenant with God (YHVH). *"A mixed multitude also went up with them, along with flocks and herds, a very large number of livestock."* (Exodus 12:38)

When God (YHVH) created Adam, he created him in absolute perfection, without sin. From Adam, God created Eve and he gave both of them free will. God created man to be in perfect, face-to-face, communication with him; however, Adam and Eve (of their own free will) chose to listen to the serpent. When they made that choice, they disobeyed God's commandment not to eat from the tree of the knowledge of good and evil, thus separating themselves from God.

> *The serpent said to the woman, "You surely will not die! For God knows that in the day you eat from it your eyes will be opened, and you will be like God, knowing good and evil." When the woman saw that the tree was good for food, and that it was a delight to the eyes, and that the tree was desirable to make one wise, she took from its fruit and ate; and she gave also to her husband with her, and he ate.* (Gen. 3:4-6)

Sin entered God's perfect creation. From Adam, sin has been passed down through all generations. *"Therefore, just as through one man sin entered into the world, and death through sin, and so death spread to all men, because all sinned"* (Rom. 5:12) From Adam to this very time, man has walked in his own understanding, wisdom and philosophies — not recognizing or acknowledging his failure to walk in God's wisdom, precepts and commandments. This is true of both Jew and gentile.

Trust in the Lord with all your heart and do not lean on your own understanding. In all your ways acknowledge Him, And He will make your paths straight. Do not be wise in your own eyes; Fear the Lord and turn away from evil. It will be healing to your body and refreshment to your bones. (Prov. 3:5-8)

God made provision for our atonement, redemption and salvation and for all our sin through the shed blood of perfect sacrificial animals.

Your lamb shall be an unblemished male a year old; you may take it from the sheep or from the goats. ... vs. 7. Moreover, they shall take some of the blood and put it on the two doorposts and on the lintel of the houses in which they eat it.... vs. 13. The blood shall be a sign for you on the houses where you live; and when I see the blood I will pass over you, and no plague will befall you to destroy you when I strike the land of Egypt...(Exod. 12:5; 7; 13)

Life is in the blood. *"'For the life of the flesh is in the blood, and I have given it to you on the altar to make atonement for your souls; for it is the blood by reason of the life that makes atonement.' "* (Lev. 17:11)

God's covenant promise to send a Savior is fulfilled is in the person of Yeshua Ha Mashiach (Jesus Christ).

> *The Lord God said to the serpent, Because you have done this, Cursed are you more than all cattle, And more than every beast of the field; On your belly you will go, And dust you will eat All the days of your life; And I will put enmity Between you and the woman, And between your seed and her seed; He shall bruise you on the head, And you shall bruise him on the heel.* (Gen. 3:14)

Also read Isaiah chapter 53 for a prophetic description of the Messiah as the perfect sacrificial Lamb who took all our sin and paid the price for our redemption. He allowed his blood to be spilled for you and for me. Yeshua is the fulfillment of God's covenant promise and provision of a redeeming savior. It is only through Yeshua that we enter into the Holy of Holies and into the presence of God. All we have to do is humble ourselves, repent of our sin, profess the name of Yeshua, and begin our lifetime commitment with God our father, Yeshua Ha Mashiach his Son, and his Ruach Ha Kodesh, his Holy Spirit. Being born again means that you have recognized, acknowledged, accepted, believed and confessed with your mouth that Yeshua Ha Mashiach is the Son of God who died, was buried and rose again from the dead.

> *If I shut up the heavens so that there is no rain, or if I command the locust to devour the land, or if I send pestilence among My people, and My people who are called by My name humble themselves and pray and seek My face and turn from their wicked ways, then I will hear from heaven, will forgive their sin and will heal their land.* (2 Chron. 7:13-14)

To "turn from" means to repent of our hardness of heart, our disobedience, rebellious actions, or anything that keeps us separated from God our father. When we do that, we are born again!

Will you cry out with a repentant heart? Will you say, "Yes, God. I want to know Your Son. I want to walk in the covenant that his blood made available to me. I receive Yeshua Ha Mashiach as my Adonai/Lord, and my redeemer. I want to walk in the power, comfort, teaching, and guidance of Your Ruach Ha Kodesh (Holy Spirit)."

If you have just made this confession, then you are born again, and have the Ruach Ha Kodesh (or Holy Spirit) living inside of you. You have become a child of God! You will find that your life and your priorities will begin to change. You will have a desire to read his Word, and his kingdom will begin to increase in your life, day by day.

The road you have now stepped onto is the highway of holiness. It is a narrow gate we walk through and a narrow path we walk since most people do not choose to go this way. *"Enter through the narrow gate; for the gate is wide and the way is broad that leads to destruction, and there are many who enter through it. For the gate is small and the way is narrow that leads to life, and there are few who find it."* (Matt. 7:13-14)

There are times when you will know his presence with such certainty and times when you will feel alone. But know this: *"...every spirit that does not confess Jesus is not from God; this is the spirit of the antichrist, of which you have heard that it is coming, and now it is already in the world. You are from God, little children, and have overcome them; because greater is He who is in you than he who is in the world."* (1 John 4:3-4) Welcome to your new life and your new family! We are each grafted into the whole house of Israel through our Jewish Savior, Yeshua Ha Mashiach. This is a lifetime commitment on earth with a promise of eternal life in heaven with our Redeemer!

CONCLUSION

I n conclusion, Proverbs tell us that it is the glory of God to hide a matter and the glory of man to search it out. (Prov. 25:2) In Hebrew the word is "dvar" (דבר). This word literally means "word," or "a matter." We have seen the word "gate" refer to a literal gate, a seat of authority and the mind. "How are you today?" could be better expressed as "How is your thinking today?" for as a man thinks or "gates" in his heart or innermost being, so is he. Who or what are you focusing on today? What are you agreeing with in your "gate" today?

In Matt. 5:17-18 Yeshua said, *"Do not think that I have come to abolish the Law or the Prophets; I have not come to abolish them, but to fulfill them. For I tell you truly, until heaven and earth pass away, not a single jot, not a stroke of a pen, will disappear from the Law until everything is accomplished."* It is interesting to note that every word, even the smallest letter, can make a world of difference in scripture. You already know how powerful words are, both the written and spoken word. In that vein I would like you to consider two words which sound the same except for the letters "p" and "v." Those words are "servant" and "serpent." Will you choose to be an instrument in the serpent's hand or to be a servant of the Most High? As stated in Proverbs 18:21, *"Death and life are in the power of the tongue, and those who love it will eat its fruit."*

Life is full of choices. Joshua 24:15 emphasizes this: *"If it is disagreeable in your sight to serve the LORD, choose for yourselves today whom you will serve: whether the gods which your fathers served which were beyond the River, or the gods of the Amorites in whose land you are living; but as for me and my house, we will serve the LORD."*

At every gate we have a choice to align ourselves with the serpent or take the role of the servant. We can come out of agreement with the enemy who wars at our gates and serve the Lord as Joshua did, or we can choose to agree with the enemy and let him have his way by submitting to his desires.

I will leave you with this thought: *"Enter through the narrow gate; for the gate is wide and the way is broad that leads to destruction, and there are many who enter through it. For the gate is small and the way is narrow that leads to life, and there are few who find it.* (Matt. 7:13-14)

Until next time....Shalom

Appendix A

RELEASING BLESSINGS AT THE GATES

Blessings at the Gate of Simeon

May _____ receive the abundant life that Messiah came to give him/her. (John 10:10)

May _____ give attention to the Word of God; and incline his/her ears to his sayings. May he/she not let them depart from his/her sight and may he/she keep them in the midst of his/her heart, for they are life to those who find them and health to all their body. (Prov. 4:20-22)

May _____ be renewed in the spirit of his/her mind, and put on the new self, which in the likeness of God has been created in righteousness and holiness of the truth. (Eph. 4:23-24)

Let _____'s mouth speak wisdom; and the meditation of his/her heart be understanding. May _____ incline his/her ear to a proverb. (Ps. 49:3-4)

May _____ love the Lord God with all his/her heart, soul, mind, and strength. (Mark 12:30)

May the Lord bless _____ with a mind set on the things above, not on the things that are on earth. (Col. 3:2)

....for the weapons of ____'s warfare are not of the flesh, but divinely powerful for the destruction of fortresses. May ____ destroy speculations and every lofty thing raised up against the knowledge of God, and may he/she take every thought captive to the obedience of Messiah. (2 Cor. 10:4-5)

And may _____ not be conformed to this world, but be transformed by the renewing of his/her mind, so that he/she may prove what the will of God is, that which is good and acceptable and perfect. (Rom. 12:2)

Blessed are ____'s eyes, because they see; and ____'s ears, because they hear. (Matt. 13:16)

You Lord, bless and keep _____ in perfect peace because his/her mind is stayed on you. (Isa. 26:3)

Blessings at the Gate of Levi

.....by the mercies of God may He enable _____ to present his/her body a living and holy sacrifice, acceptable to God, which is ____'s spiritual service of worship. (Rom. 12:1)

May the God of Abraham, Isaac and Jacob bless ____ so that he/she may be blameless before him. (Deut. 18:13)

May ____ walk before the Lord as Noah who was a righteous man, blameless in his time. (Gen. 6:9)

May no unwholesome word proceed from ____'s mouth, but only such a word as is good for edification according to the need of the moment, so that it will give grace to those who hear. (Eph. 4:29)

May _____ never practice witchcraft and use divination, or associate with mediums and spiritists. (2 Kings 21:6)

May _____ walk after the spirit and not after the flesh that he/she will remain free from condemnation. (Rom. 8:1)

May _____ deny ungodliness and worldly desires and live sensibly, righteously and godly in the present age. (Titus 2:12)

May the Lord send out His light and His truth, and let them lead _____; Let them bring _____ to Your holy hill and to Your dwelling places. (Ps. 43:3)

May _____ be a true disciple of the God of Abraham, Isaac, and Jacob and know the truth, and the truth will make him/her free. (John 8:32)

May the Spirit of truth guide _____ into all the truth; for He will not speak on His own initiative, but whatever He hears, He will speak; and He will disclose to _____ what is to come. (John 16:13)

Blessings at the Gate of Judah

May _____'s footsteps be established in your Word, and do not let any iniquity have dominion over him/her. (Ps. 119:133)

May the Lord make his face to shine upon _____, and teach him/her his statutes. (Ps. 119:135)

May _____ have more insight than all of his/her teachers, May your testimonies be his/her meditation. (Ps. 119:99)

May _____ observe your precepts so that he/she may understand more than the aged. (Ps. 119: 99-100)

May your Word be a lamp to _____'s feet and a light to his/her path. (Ps. 119:105)

May the Lord bless _____ with a hunger and thirst for righteousness, so that he/she shall be satisfied. (Matt. 5:6)

May the Lord bless _____ as he/she walks in all the way which the Lord his/her God has commanded, that he/she may live and that it may be well with him/her, and that he/she may prolong his/her days in the land which he/she will possess. (Deut. 5:33)

May this book of the law not depart from _____'s mouth, but may he/she meditate on it day and night, so that he/she may be careful to do according to all that is written in it; for then he/she will make his/her way prosperous, and he/she will have success. (Josh. 1:8)

"May _____ love the Lord his/her God with all his/her heart, and with all his/her soul, and with all his/her strength, and with all his/her mind; and his/her neighbor as himself/herself." (Luke 10:27)

May _____ submit therefore to God. May _____ resist the devil so that he will flee from him/her. May _____ draw near to God so that he will draw near to _____. (James 4:7, 8)

Blessings at the Gate of Issachar

May _____ overcome by the blood of the Lamb, and by the word of his/her testimony; and not love his/her life unto the death. (Rev. 12:11)

Blessed is _____ that endureth temptation: for when he/she is tried, he/she shall receive the crown of life, which the LORD hath promised to those that love Him. (James 1:12)

Blessed is _____. May he/she always and at all times hunger and thirst for righteousness, for he/she shall be filled. (Matt. 5:6)

May _____ seek first the kingdom of God and His righteousness, so that all these things shall be given to him/her. (Matt. 6:33)

May _____ as a sojourner and exile abstain from the passions of the flesh, which wage war against his/her soul. (1 Pet. 2:11)

May God who is faithful, not let _____ be tempted beyond his/her ability, but with the temptation he will also provide the way of escape, that he/she may be able to endure it. (1 Cor. 10:13)

Father, let grace enable _____ to put to death what is earthly in him/her: sexual immorality, impurity, passion, evil desire, and covetousness, which is idolatry. (Col. 3:5)

May _____ walk by the Spirit, and not gratify the desires of the flesh. (Gal. 5:16)

May _____ set his/her mind on the things of the spirit and not those things of the flesh. (Rom. 8:5)

Let _____ do nothing from selfishness or empty conceit, but with humility of mind regard others as more important than himself/herself. (Phil. 2:3)

Blessings at the Gate of Joseph

May _____ diligently hearken to the voice of the LORD God and do that which is right in his sight and give ear to his commandments and keep all his statutes; then He will put none of these diseases upon him/her which He has brought upon the Egyptians for He is the LORD that heals him/her. (Exod. 15:26)

_____ shall serve the LORD his/her God and he shall bless his/her bread and water and take sickness away from the midst of him/her. (Exod. 23:25-26)

And the LORD will take away from _____ all sickness and will put none of the evil diseases of Egypt, which you know, upon him/her, but will lay them upon all them that hate him/her. (Deut. 7:15)

Because _____ has made the LORD, his/her refuge, even the most High, his/her habitation; There shall no evil befall him/her, neither shall any plague come nigh his/her dwelling. (Ps. 91:9-10)

May ____ bless the LORD at all times and not forget all of his benefits. May the Lord forgive all _____'s iniquities and heal all his/her diseases; may He redeem his/her life from destruction and crown him/her with lovingkindness and tender mercies and satisfy his/her mouth with good things; so that his/her youth is renewed like the eagle's. (Ps. 103:1-5)

May _____ eat your Word daily. May it continually flow in his/her bloodstream. May it flow to every cell of his/her body, restoring and transforming his/her body. Your Word, O Lord has become flesh; for You sent Your Word and healed _____. (Ps. 107:20)

May the Lord send his word to _____ and heal and deliver him/her from his/her destructions. (Ps. 107:19-20)

And these signs shall follow _____ because he/she believes; In my name he/she shall cast out devils; speak with new tongues; take up serpents; and if he/she drinks any deadly thing, it shall not hurt him/her. He/She shall lay hands on the sick, and they shall recover. (Mark 16:17-18)

"Beloved, I wish above all things that _____ mayest prosper and be in health, even as his/her soul prospers. (3 John 2)

May the life through the word of God flow to every organ and tissue of _____'s body bringing healing and health.

Blessings at the Gate of Benjamin

May ____ humble himself/herself before the Lord, and be lifted up in every circumstance in his/her life. (James 4:10)

May the Lord clothe _____ with compassion, kindness, humility, gentleness and patience as God's chosen people, holy and dearly loved. (Col. 3:12)

May ____ have the patience for God to lift him/her up after he/she has humbled himself/herself, under God's mighty hand. (1 Pet 4:6)

Holy Spirit, help _____ to act justly and to love mercy, and to walk humbly with his/her God. (Micah 6:8)

Let _____ be completely humble and gentle; be patient, bearing with one another in love. (Eph. 4:2)

Holy Spirit help _____ live in harmony with others. Help him/her to not be proud, but be willing to associate with people of low position, and not be conceited. (Rom. 12:16)

May the Lord keep _____ from being a lover of self, a lover of money, proud, arrogant, abusive, disobedient to his/her parents, ungrateful, unholy, heartless, unappeasable, slanderous, without self-control, brutal, not loving good, treacherous, reckless, swollen with conceit, a lover of pleasure rather than a lover of God, having the appearance of godliness, but denying its power as many will be in the last days. (2 Tim. 3:1-5)

May the Lord turn away ____'s eyes from looking at vanity, and revive him/her in His ways. (Ps. 119:37)

Lord let ____learn from those who did not obey or incline their ear, but walked in their own counsels and in the stubbornness of their evil heart, and went backward and not forward. (Jer. 7:24)

May _____ be blessed because he/she hears the Word of God and observes it. (Luke 11:28)

Blessings at the Gate of Reuben

May the blood of the Lamb of God, slain from the foundation of the world cleanse, wash, and release forgiveness for _____ as I bring him/her before you at the Gate of Reuben. (Rev. 13:8)

May _____'s iniquities no longer separate him/her from his/her God, because of the blood of the Lamb. (Isa. 59:2)

May _____'s sins which have been as scarlet, be white as snow. (Isa. 1:18)

May _____ rejoice when persecuted because of righteousness, for his/hers is the kingdom of heaven. (Matt. 5:10)

When people insult _____, persecute him/her and falsely say all kinds of evil against him/her because of me, may _____ rejoice and be glad, because great is his/her reward in heaven, for in the same way they persecuted the prophets who were before him/her. (Matt. 5:11)

May _____ not be taken captive through philosophy and empty deception, according to the tradition of men. (Col. 2:8)

I decree and declare at the Gate of Reuben that _____ is covered with the blood of Yeshua and no longer walks just as the Gentiles also walk, in the futility of their mind. (Eph. 4:17)

May _____'s mind no longer be hardened; and at the reading of the Old Covenant let the veil be lifted, because it is removed in Messiah. (2 Cor. 3:15)

May _____ not be controlled by his/her sinful nature. May he/she walk by the spirit and not carry out the desire of the flesh. (Gal. 5:16)

May all of the gifts of the spirit flow freely through _____ and may the fruit of the Spirit mature and be abundant in _____'s life. (Gal. 5:22)

Blessings at the Gate of Gad

May the Lord God of Israel bless _____ with love, power, and a sound mind. (2 Tim. 1:7)

The LORD is _____'s light and salvation— whom shall he/she fear? The LORD is the stronghold of his/her life— of whom shall he/she be afraid? (Ps. 27:1)

May the Lord bless _____ with strength and courage. _____, do not be afraid; do not be discouraged, for the LORD his/her God will be with him/her wherever he/she goes. (Josh. 1:9)

May the Lord keep _____ in perfect peace, as his/her mind is stayed on thee: because he/she trusts in thee. (Isa. 26:3)

May the fear of the LORD be _____'s portion as it tendeth to life: and he/she shall abide satisfied; and not be visited with evil. (Prov. 19:23)

May _____ be anxious for nothing, but in everything by prayer and supplication with thanksgiving let his/her requests be made known to God. And the peace of God, which surpasses all comprehension, will guard his/her heart and mind in Christ Jesus. (Phil. 4:6-7)

May _____ put his/her trust in God when he/she is afraid. (Ps. 56:3)

May the Lord prosper _____ and may he/she be in health even as his/her soul prospers. (3 John 2)

May _____ all the days of his/her life dwell in the shelter of the Most High and abide in the shadow of the Almighty. (Ps. 91:1)

May _____ walk uprightly all the days of his/her life that he/she may receive grace and glory and all good things. (Ps. 84:11)

Blessings at the Gate of Asher

Now may the God of hope fill _____ with all joy and peace in believing, that he/she may abound in hope, through the power of the Holy Spirit. (Rom. 15:13)

May _____ wait upon the LORD so that he/she shall renew his/her strength; so that he/she shall mount up with wings as eagles; shall run, and not be weary; and shall walk, and not faint. (Isa. 40:31)

May _____ be blessed because he/she trusts in the LORD, and his/her hope is in the LORD. (Jer. 17:7)

May _____be strong and of a good courage, fear not, nor be afraid of them: for the LORD thy God, he [it is] that goes with him/her; he will not fail him/her, nor forsake him/her. (Deut. 31:6)

May the Lord grant _____ the oil of gladness instead of mourning, the mantle of praise instead of a spirit of fainting. (Isa. 61:3)

May _____ rejoice greatly in the Lord, may _____'s soul exult in God; for he has clothed him/her with garments of salvation, he has wrapped him/her with a robe of righteousness. (Isa. 61:10)

May the Lord make known to _____ the path of life; In Your presence is fullness of joy; In Your right hand there are pleasures forever. (Ps. 16:11)

May _____ hear and serve him, so that he/she will end his/her days in prosperity and his/her years in pleasures. (Job 36:11)

May the Lord make _____ most blessed forever; May the Lord make him/her joyful with gladness in His presence. (Ps. 21:6)

May the Lord hear _____ when he/she cries, and deliver him/her out of all his/her troubles. (Ps. 34:17)

Blessings at the Gate of Zebulon

May _____ repent from or never turn to mediums or spiritists; may he/she never seek them out to be defiled by them. I am the LORD _____'s God. (Lev. 19:31)

May there be repentance from or never be found among _____'s descendants anyone who makes his/her son or daughter to pass through the fire, uses divination, practices witchcraft, or interprets omens, or a sorcerer, that the Lord may bless and hear him/her when he/she calls. (Deut. 18:10)

May _____ repent from or never turn to mediums and to spiritists, to play the harlot after them, so that God will not set His face against him/her. _____ shall consecrate himself/herself and be holy, for I am the LORD his/her God. _____ shall keep My statutes and practice them; I am the LORD who sanctifies him/her. (Lev. 20: 6, 7)

May _____ be like Josiah who removed the mediums and the spiritists and the teraphim and the idols and all the abominations that were seen in the land of Judah and in Jerusalem that he/she might confirm the words of the law which were written in the book that Hilkiah the priest found in the house of the LORD. (2 Kings 23:24)

May _____ never forsake all the commandments of the LORD his/her God and make for himself/herself molten images, but worship the Lord and serve him all the days of his/her life. (2 Kings 17:16)

May the Lord create in _____ a clean heart, and renew a steadfast spirit within him/her. (Ps. 51:10)

Therefore, having these promises, beloved, let ____ cleanse himself/ herself from all defilement of flesh and spirit, perfecting holiness in the fear of God. (2 Cor. 7:1)

May ____ repent from and abstain from every form of evil. (1 Thess. 5:22)

May the Lord cause ____ to repent from and abstain from fleshly lusts which wage war against the soul. (1 Pet. 2:11)

May ____ be strong in the Lord and in the strength of His might. May ____ put on the full armor of God, so that he/she will be able to stand firm against the schemes of the devil. May he/she remember that our struggle is not against flesh and blood, but against the rulers, against the powers, against the world forces of this darkness, against the spiritual forces of wickedness in the heavenly places. (Eph. 6:10-12)

Blessings at the Gate of Dan

May the Lord which has shown ____ great and sore troubles, quicken him/her again, and bring him/her up again from the depths of the earth. (Ps. 71:20)

May ____ never come short of the grace of God; lest any root of bitterness spring up to trouble him/her, and thereby many be defiled. (Heb. 12:15)

No temptation has taken ____ but such as is common to man: but God is faithful, who will bless him/her by not allowing him/her to be tempted above that which he/she is able; but will with the temptation also make a way to escape, that he/she may be able to bear it. (1 Cor. 10:13)

All things are lawful to _____, but all things are not expedient: all things are lawful for him/her, but he/she will not be brought under the power of any. (1 Cor. 6:12)

May God who pardons sin and forgives the transgression of the remnant of his inheritance not stay angry with _____ but delight to show mercy. You will again have compassion on him/her and you will tread his/her sins underfoot and hurl all iniquities into the depths of the sea. (Mic. 7:18, 19)

Blessed is _____ because he/she has quickly sought the favor of the LORD his/her God by turning from his/her iniquity and giving attention to your truth therefore avoiding calamity. (Dan. 9:13)

May the LORD be near to and bless _____ because he/she has a broken heart, and a contrite spirit. (Ps. 34:18)

May the Lord give justice to _____ because he/she is weak and fatherless; May He also heal and/or sustain him/her because of the affliction he/she is suffering from, and the destitute situation he/she finds himself/herself in. May you be a very present help in time of trouble for _____. (Ps. 82:3)

Let _____ call upon You in the day of trouble; he/she is blessed as You O God are his/her deliverer. He/she will glorify You! (Ps. 50: 15)

Blessed is _____ because he/she heeds your voice, and accepts instruction. He/she also trusts in the LORD, and he/she draws near to his/her God. (Deut. 32:17-18)

Blessings at the Gate of Naphtali

Let _____'s love be without hypocrisy. May _____ abhor what is evil; and cling to what is good. (Rom. 12:9)

May _____ always and at all times bless those who persecute him/her; and not curse. (Rom. 12:14)

May _____ always remember he/she is chosen of God, holy and beloved. May _____ put on a heart of compassion, kindness, humility, gentleness and patience; bearing with others, and forgiving others, beyond all these things may he/she put on love, which is the perfect bond of unity. (Col. 3:12-14)

May _____ honor all people, love the brotherhood, fear God, and honor the king. (1 Pet. 2:17)

Father pour out your love on _____ and let him/her love others, for love is from God; and everyone who loves is born of God and knows God. (1 John 4:7)

May _____ be filled with the fruit of the Spirit which is love, joy, peace, patience, kindness, goodness, faithfulness, gentleness, self-control; against such things there is no law. (Gal. 5:22)

May _____ be quick to hear, slow to speak and slow to anger. (James 1:19)

May _____ guard his/her mouth and his/her tongue, therefore guarding his/her soul from troubles. (Prov. 21:23)

May _____ not speak harsh words which stir up anger, but instead always give a gentle answer which turns away wrath. (Prov. 15:1)

Father, Let no unwholesome word proceed from _____'s mouth, but only such a word as is good for edification according to the need of the moment, so that it will give grace to those who hear. (Eph. 4:29)

Appendix B

STRONGHOLDS/REDEMPTIVE KEYS

Let's take a look at which tribes released the blessing and which tribes released the curses and why they were chosen to do so. As we do, we will understand the redemptive keys that are released at the particular gates and discover that some of them are used to release the blessing and some to restrain the curse.

First, here are the tribes who proclaimed the blessings on Mt. Gerazim along with scriptures that illuminate the blessings which were released. The redemptive keys at these gates release the blessings.

Gate of Simeon—"Hearing"	
Stronghold: Deaf & Mute Spirit	Manifestations: Blindness, Can't function, Convulsions, Deafness, Muteness, Ear disease, Epilepsy, Eye disease, Foaming mouth, Insanity, Lunacy, Pining away, Schizophrenia, Seizures, Suicide, Tearing
Redemptive Key – Fasting	
"Is this not the fast which I choose, To loosen the bonds of wickedness, To undo the bands of the yoke, And to let the oppressed go free And break every yoke? Is it not to divide your bread with the hungry And bring the homeless poor into the house; When you see the naked, to cover him; And not to hide yourself from your own flesh? Then your light will break out like the dawn, And your recovery will speedily spring forth; And your righteousness will go before you; The glory of the Lord will be your rear guard. Then you will call, and the Lord will answer; You will cry, and He will say, 'Here I am.' If you remove the yoke from your midst, The pointing of the finger and speaking wickedness, And if you give yourself to the hungry And satisfy the desire of the afflicted, Then your light will rise in darkness And your gloom will become like midday. And the Lord will continually guide you, And satisfy your desire in scorched places, And give strength to your bones; And you will be like a watered garden, And like a spring of water whose waters do not fail." (Isa. 58:6-11)	

Gate of Levi–"Joined" or "Joint Heir"	
Stronghold: Lying Spirit	Manifestations: Adultery, Condemnation, Divination, Exaggeration, Fornication, Homosexuality, Hypocrisy/Delusion, Profanity, Religious spirit, Sodomy, Superstition, Vanity, Witchcraft
Redemptive Key: Word	

"So will My word be which goes forth from My mouth; It will not return to Me empty, Without accomplishing what I desire, And without succeeding in the matter for which I sent it." (Isa. 5:11)

"Your word I have treasured in my heart, That I may not sin against You."

(Ps. 119:11)

"Is not My word like fire?" declares the Lord, *"and like a hammer which shatters a rock?"* (Jer. 23:29)

Gate of Judah–"Let God be Praised"	
<u>Stronghold</u>: Perversion (produces hatred of Yahweh)	<u>Manifestations</u>: Doctrinal Error, Error, Hate, Hatred of God, Homosexuality, Lust, Pervert/Gospel, Rebellion, Self-Lovers, Sexual Troubles, Twist Truth, Wounded Spirit, Wrong Teaching

Redemptive Key: Holiness
"Do not be bound together with unbelievers; for what partnership have righteousness and lawlessness, or what fellowship has light with darkness? Or what harmony has Christ with Belial, or what has a believer in common with an unbeliever? Or what agreement has the temple of God with idols? For we are the temple of the living God; just as God said, "I will dwell in them and walk among them; And I will be their God, and they shall be My people. Therefore, come out from their midst and be separate," says the Lord. "And do not touch what is unclean; And I will welcome you. And I will be a father to you, And you shall be sons and daughters to Me," Says the Lord Almighty." (2 Cor. 6:14-18)

Gate of Issachar–"Man of Hire"	
<u>Stronghold</u>: Whoredom (serving money, the world)	<u>Manifestations</u>: Adultery, All sexual sin, Emotionally weak, Fornication, Homosexuality, Idolatry, Love of money, Love of the world, Pornography, Prostitution, Unclean/foul, Unequally yoked
Redemptive Key: Giving	

"Bring the whole tithe into the storehouse, so that there may be food in My house, and test Me now in this," says the Lord of hosts, "if I will not open for you the windows of heaven and pour out for you a blessing until it overflows." (Mal. 3:10)

"Heal the sick, raise the dead, cleanse the lepers, cast out demons. Freely you received, freely give." (Matt. 10:8)

"Now He who supplies seed to the sower and bread for food will supply and multiply your seed for sowing and increase the harvest of your righteousness." (2 Cor. 9:10)

Gate of Joseph–"One who Increases"	
<u>Stronghold</u>: Infirmity	<u>Manifestations</u>: All sickness, Arthritis, Asthma, Bone problems, Cancer, Colds, Ear problems, Fever, Heart problems, Hunchback, Lung problems, Muscle problems, Sinus problems, Viruses, Weakness
Redemptive Key: Worship	

"Because Your lovingkindness is better than life, My lips will praise You. So I will bless You as long as I live; I will lift up my hands in Your name." (Ps. 63:3-4)

"Blessed be the Lord, who daily bears our burden, The God who is our salvation. Selah." (Ps. 68:19)

"But as for me, I shall sing of Your strength; Yes, I shall joyfully sing of Your lovingkindness in the morning, For You have been my stronghold And a refuge in the day of my distress." (Ps. 59:16)

Gate of Benjamin—"Son of my Right Hand"	
<u>Stronghold</u>: Pride	<u>Manifestations</u>: Arrogance, Contention, Control Spirit, Dictatorial, Egotistical, Gossip, Haughtiness, Mockery, Pride, Scorn, Self-righteousness, Stubbornness, Vanity, Wrath
Redemptive Key: Humility	

"[If]… My people who are called by My name humble themselves and pray and seek My face and turn from their wicked ways, then I will hear from heaven, will forgive their sin and will heal their land." (Isa. 7:14)

"And when he humbled himself, the anger of the Lord turned away from him, so as not to destroy him completely; and also conditions were good in Judah." (2 Chron. 12:12)

"For the Lord takes pleasure in his people; he adorns the humble with salvation." (Ps. 149:4 English Standard Version [ESV])

Now let's look at the redemptive keys which restrained the curses released on Mount Ebal by the second group of tribes. Since Yeshua became a curse for us, we can release these redemptive keys which are blessings that restrain the curse!

Gate of Reuben—"Behold the Son"	
<u>Stronghold</u>: Anti-Christ Spirit	<u>Manifestations</u>: Against Christ, Lawlessness, Atheism, Blasphemies, Controlling spirit, Humanism, Legalism, New Age, Opposing men of God, Persecution of the saints, Self-appointed, Speaks against gifts of the Spirit, Substituting the blood, Super spiritual ministries
Redemptive Key: Blood of Messiah	

"The blood shall be a sign for you on the houses where you live; and when I see the blood I will pass over you, and no plague will befall you to destroy you when I strike the land of Egypt." (Exod. 12:13)
"For the life of the flesh is in the blood, and I have given it to you on the altar to make atonement for your souls; for it is the blood by reason of the life that makes atonement." (Lev. 17:11)
"And according to the Law, one may almost say, all things are cleansed with blood, and without shedding of blood there is no forgiveness." (Heb. 9:22)
"[But you have come]... to Jesus, the mediator of a new covenant, and to the sprinkled blood, which speaks better than the blood of Abel." (Heb. 12:24)

Gate of Gad–"Good Fortune"	
<u>Stronghold</u>: Spirit of Fear	<u>Manifestations</u>: Anxiety, Cancer, Heart problems, Fear of heights, Horror, Inadequacy, Inferiority, Nightmares, Poverty, Sensing Danger, Tension/Stress, Think the worst, Timidity, Torment, Worry
Redemptive Key: Faith	
"... in addition to all, taking up the shield of faith with which you will be able to extinguish all the flaming arrows of the evil one." (Eph. 6:16) *"He who has believed and has been baptized shall be saved; but he who has disbelieved shall be condemned."* (Mark 16:16) *"And without faith it is impossible to please Him, for he who comes to God must believe that He is and that He is a rewarder of those who seek Him."* (Heb. 11:6)	

Gate of Asher—"Happy"	
<u>Stronghold</u>: Spirit of Heaviness	<u>Manifestations</u>: Depression, Despair, Discouragement, Gloominess, Gluttony, Grief, Hopelessness, Idolatry, Loneliness, Mourning, Rejection, Sadness, Self-pity, Sorrow, Troubles
Redemptive Key: Praise	
"When he had consulted with the people, he appointed those who sang to the Lord and those who praised Him in holy attire, as they went out before the army and said, 'Give thanks to the Lord, for His lovingkindness is everlasting.' When they began singing and praising, the Lord set ambushes against the sons of Ammon, Moab and Mount Seir, who had come against Judah; so they were routed." (2 Chron. 20:21-22) *"Let the high praises of God be in their mouth, And a two-edged sword in their hand, To execute vengeance on the nations And punishment on the peoples,* *To bind their kings with chains And their nobles with fetters of iron..."* (Ps. 149:6-8)	

Gate of Zebulon–"Dwelling"	
<u>Stronghold</u>: Familiar Spirits	<u>Manifestations</u>: Astrology, Demonic sounds, Divination, ESP, Fortune telling, Horoscope, Hypnosis, Music beats, New Age, Occult, Psychic ability, Smells-incense, Witchcraft
Redemptive Key: Repentance	

"Therefore repent and return, so that your sins may be wiped away, in order that times of refreshing may come from the presence of the Lord..." (Acts 3:19)

"The Lord is not slow about His promise, as some count slowness, but is patient toward you, not wishing for any to perish but for all to come to repentance." (2 Pet. 3:9)

"'Therefore I will judge you, O house of Israel, each according to his conduct,' declares the Lord God. 'Repent and turn away from all your transgressions, so that iniquity may not become a stumbling block to you. Cast away from you all your transgressions which you have committed and make yourselves a new heart and a new spirit! For why will you die, O house of Israel? For I have no pleasure in the death of anyone who dies,' declares the Lord God. 'Therefore, repent and live.'" (Ezek. 18:30-32)

Gate of Dan—"Judge"	
<u>Stronghold</u>: Bondage	<u>Manifestations</u>: Abused/Broken, Addictions, Alcohol, Anguish, Bitterness, Cancer, Cigarettes, Compulsive, Drugs, Greed, Lust, Prayerlessness, Satanic activity, Spiritual blindness, Unforgiving
Redemptive Key: Holy Spirit	
"For the law of the Spirit of life in Christ Jesus has set you free from the law of sin and of death. For what the Law could not do, weak as it was through the flesh, God did: sending His own Son in the likeness of sinful flesh and as an offering for sin, He condemned sin in the flesh, so that the requirement of the Law might be fulfilled in us, who do not walk according to the flesh but according to the Spirit. For those who are according to the flesh set their minds on the things of the flesh, but those who are according to the Spirit, the things of the Spirit. For the mind set on the flesh is death, but the mind set on the Spirit is life and peace..." (Rom. 8:2-6)	

Gate of Naphtali—"My Wrestling"	
<u>Stronghold</u>: Jealousy	<u>Manifestations</u>: Adultery, Anger, Competition, Cruelty, Division, Envy, Murder, Rage, Restlessness, Revenge, Selfishness, Suspicion, Wrath
Redemptive Key: Love	

"Above all, keep fervent in your love for one another, because love covers a multitude of sins." (1 Pet. 4:8)

"For God so loved the world, that He gave His only begotten Son, that whoever believes in Him shall not perish, but have eternal life." (John 3:16)

"There is no fear in love; but perfect love casts out fear, because fear involves punishment, and the one who fears is not perfected in love." (1 John 4:18)

"Beloved, let us love one another, for love is from God; and everyone who loves is born of God and knows God. The one who does not love does not know God, for God is love." (1 John 4:7-8)

Appendix C

SUPPORTING SCRIPTURES FOR STRONGHOLDS

The Gate of Simeon/Deaf and Mute Spirit

MATTHEW 15:10
"And after He called the multitude to him, He said to them, Hear, and understand."

JOHN 10:3
"To him the doorkeeper opens, and the sheep hear his voice, and he calls his own sheep by name, and leads them out."

JOHN 10:27
"My sheep hear My voice, and I know them, and they follow Me."

MATTHEW 11:15
"He who has ears to hear let him hear."

JOHN 5:24
"Truly, truly, I say to you, he who hears My word, and believes Him who sent Me, has eternal life, and does not come into judgement, but has passed out of death into life."

JAMES 1:19
"This you know, my beloved brethren, but let everyone be quick to hear, slow to speak, and slow to anger;"

ROMANS 10:17
"So faith comes from hearing and hearing by the word of Christ."

PROVERBS 20:12
"The hearing ear and the seeing eye, The Lord has made both of them."

HEBREWS 5:11
"Concerning him we have much to say, and it is hard to explain, since you have become dull of hearing."

PSALM 66:18
"If I regard wickedness in my heart, The Lord will not hear; but certainly God has heard; He has given heed to the voice of my prayer."

1 JOHN 5:14-15
"And this is the confidence which we have before Him, that, if we ask anything according to His will, He hears us. And if we know that He hears us in whatever we ask, we know that we have the requests which we have asked from Him."

MARK 8:18
"'Having eyes do you not see? And having ears do you not hear? And do you not remember when I broke the five loaves, for the five thousand, how many baskets full of broken pieces you picked up?' They said to Him, 'Twelve.'"

The Gate of Levi/Lying Spirit

ZECHARIAH 8:16
'These are the things which you should do: speak the truth to one another; judge with truth and judgments for peace in your gates."

ZECHARIAH 8:3
"Thus says the LORD, I will return to Zion and will dwell in the midst of Jerusalem. Then Jerusalem will be called the City of Truth, and the mountain of the LORD of Hosts will be called the Holy Mountain."

PROVERBS 12:17
"He who speaks truth tells what is right, But a false witness deceit."

PROVERBS 3:3-4
"Do not let kindness and truth leave you; Bind them around your neck, Write them on the tablet of your heart. So you will find favor and good repute in the sight of God and man."

ROMANS 3:4
"May it never be! Rather, let God be found true, though every man be found a liar,"

JOHN 8:31-32
"If you abide in My word, then you are truly disciples of Mine; and you shall know the truth, and the truth shall make you free."

JOHN 14:6
"I am the way, and the truth, and the life; no one comes to the Father but through Me."

ROMANS 1:25
"For they exchanged the truth of God for a lie, and worshipped and served the creature rather than the Creator who is blessed forever. Amen."

PROVERBS 19:5
"A false witness will not go unpunished, and he who tells lies will not escape."

COLOSSIANS 3: 9-10
"Do not lie to one another, since you laid aside the old self, with its evil practices and have put on the new self who is being renewed to a true knowledge according to the image of the One who created him."

COLOSSIANS 2:8
"See to it that no one takes you captive through philosophy and empty deception, according to the tradition of men, according to the elementary principles of the world, rather than according to Christ."

REVELATION 21:8
"But for the cowardly and unbelieving and abominable and murderers and immoral persons and sorcerers and idolaters and all liars, their part will be in the lake that burns with fire and brimstone, which is the second death."

The Gate of Judah/Spirit of Perversion

COLOSSIANS 2:8
"See to it that no one takes you captive through philosophy and empty deception, according to the tradition of men, according to the elementary principles of the world, rather than according to Christ."

LUKE 3:4-6
"The voice of one crying in the wilderness, Make ready the way of the LORD. Make his paths straight. Every ravine shall be filled up and every mountain and hill shall be brought low; and the crooked shall become straight, and the rough roads smooth; and all flesh shall see the salvation of GOD."

ISAIAH 2:3
"And many peoples will come and say, Come, let us go up to the mountain of the Lord, to the house of the God of Jacob. That He may teach us concerning his ways, and that we may walk in His paths."

PSALM 1:1
"How blessed is the man who does not walk in the counsel of the wicked, nor stand in the path of sinners, nor sit in the seat of scoffers! But his delight is in the law of the LORD and in his law he meditates day and night."

PSALM 119:105
"Your word is a lamp to my feet and a light to my path."

PSALM 139:23-24
"Search me, O God, and know my heart; Try me and know my anxious thoughts; and see if there be any hurtful way in me and lead me in the everlasting way."

PROV 3:5-6
"Trust in the Lord with all of your heart, and do not lean on your own understanding. In all your ways acknowledge Him and He will make your paths straight."

1 CORINTHIANS 6:13
"...Yet the body is not meant for immorality but for the Lord and the Lord for the body."

1 CORINTHIANS 6:18-20
"Flee immorality. Every other sin that a man commits is outside his body, but the immoral man sins against his own body. For you have been bought with a price: therefore glorify God in your body."

PSALM 19:12
"Who can discern his errors? Acquit me of hidden faults."

DEUTERONOMY 23:14

"Since the LORD your God walks in the midst of your camp to deliver you and to defeat your enemies before you, therefore your camp must be holy; and He must not see anything indecent among you lest he turn away from you."

EZEKIEL 36:25-27

"Then I will sprinkle clean water on you, and you will be clean; I will cleanse you from all of your filthiness and from all of your idols. Moreover, I will give you a new heart and put a new spirit within you; and I will remove the heart of stone from your flesh and give you a heart of flesh. And I will put My Spirit within you and I will cause you to walk in My statutes and you will be careful to observe My ordinances."

The Gate of Issachar/Spirit of Whoredom

1 JOHN 2:15-16

"Do not love the world nor the things in the world. If anyone loves the world, the love of the Father is not in him. For all that is in the world, the lust of the flesh and the lust of the eyes, and the boastful pride of life, is not from the Father, but is from the world."

1 THESSALONIANS 4:3-5

"For this is the will of God, your sanctification; that is, that you abstain from sexual immorality; that each of you know how to possess his own vessel in sanctification and honor, not in lustful passion, like the Gentiles who do not know God."

1 CORINTHIANS 6: 16-20

"Or do you not know that the one who joins himself to a harlot is one body with her? For He says the two will become one flesh. But the one who joins himself to the Lord is one spirit with Him. Flee immorality. Every other sin that a man commits is outside the body, but the immoral man sins against his own body. Or do you not know that your body is a temple of the Holy Spirit who is in you, whom you have from God, and that you are not your own? For you have been bought with a price therefore glorify God in your body."

COLOSSIANS 3:5
"Therefore consider the members of your earthly body as dead to immorality, impurity, passion, evil desire, and greed, which amounts to idolatry."

1 CORINTHIANS 10:7-8
"And do not be idolaters, as some of them were; Nor let us act immorally, as some of them did and twenty-three thousand fell in one day."

ROMANS 12:1-2
"I urge you therefore, brethren, by the mercies of God, to present your bodies a living and holy sacrifice, acceptable to God, which is your spiritual service of worship. And do not be conformed to this world, but be transformed by the renewing of your mind, that you may prove what the will of God is, that which is good and acceptable and perfect."

ISAIAH 35:8
"A highway will be there, a roadway, and it will be called the Highway of Holiness.

The unclean will not travel on it, but it will be for him who walks that way, and fools will not wander on it."

The Gate of Joseph/Spirit of Infirmity

JEREMIAH 17:14
"Heal me, O Lord, and I will be healed; Save me and I will be saved, for You are my praise."

EXODUS 15:26

"And He said, If you will give earnest heed to the voice of the LORD your God, and do what is right in His sight, and give ear to His commandments, and keep all His statutes, I will put none of the diseases on you which I have put on the Egyptians, for I, the LORD am your healer."

DEUTERONOMY 7:15

"And the Lord will remove from you all sickness; and He will not put on you any of the harmful diseases of Egypt which you have known, but He will lay them on all who hate you."

EXODUS 23:25

"But you shall serve the LORD your God, and He will bless your bread and your water; and I will remove sickness from your midst."

PROVERBS 3:7-8

"Do not be wise in your own eyes; Fear the LORD and turn away from evil. It will be healing to your body, and refreshment to your bones."

PROVERBS 4:20-22

"My son, give attention to my words; Incline your ear to my sayings. Do not let them depart from your sight; Keep them in the midst of your heart. For they are life to those who find them, and health to all their whole body."

PSALM 103:1-5

"Bless the LORD, O my soul; And all that is within me, bless His holy name. Bless the LORD, O my soul and forget none of His benefits. Who pardons all of your iniquities; Who heals all your diseases; Who redeems your life from the pit; who crowns you with lovingkindness and compassion; Who satisfies your years with good things so that your youth is renewed like the eagle."

3 JOHN 2

"Beloved, I pray that in all respects you may prosper and be in good health, just as your soul prospers."

ACTS 10:38

"You know of Jesus of Nazareth, how God anointed Him with the Holy Spirit, and with power, and how He went about doing good, and healing all who were oppressed by the devil, for God was with Him."

MATTHEW 8:16-17

"And when evening had come, they brought to Him many who were demon-possessed; and He cast out the spirits with a word, and healed all who were ill in order that what was spoken through Isaiah the prophet might be fulfilled, saying, He Himself took our infirmities and carried away our diseases."

MATTHEW 9:35

"And Jesus was going about all the cities and the villages, teaching in their synagogues and proclaiming the gospel of the kingdom, and healing every kind of disease and every kind of sickness."

MARK 16:17-18

"And these signs will accompany those who have believed: in My name they will cast out demons, they will speak with new tongues; they will pick up serpents, and if they drink any deadly poison, it shall not hurt them; they will lay hands on the sick, and they will recover."

The Gate of Benjamin/Spirit of Pride

MICAH 6:8

"...and what does the Lord require of you But to do justice, to love kindness, and to walk humbly with your God."

2 CHRONICLES 34:27

"Because your heart was tender and you humbled yourself before God, when you heard His words against this place and against its inhabitants, and because you humbled yourself before Me, tore your clothes, and wept before Me, I truly have heard you," declares the LORD."

JOEL 2:13a
"...And rend your hearts and not your garments."

2 CHRONICLES 7:14
"...and my people who are called by my name humble themselves and pray, and seek my face, and turn from their wicked ways, then I will hear from heaven, will forgive their sin, and will heal their land."

JAMES 4:6
"But He gives a greater grace. Therefore it says, God is opposed to the proud, but gives grace to the humble."

JAMES 4:10
"Humble yourselves in the presence of the Lord and He will exalt you."

1 PETER 5:6
"Humble yourselves, therefore, under the mighty hand of God, that He may exalt you at the proper time."

PROVERBS 16:18
"Pride goes before destruction, and a haughty spirit before stumbling."

PROVERBS 8:13
"The fear of the LORD is to hate evil; pride and arrogance and the evil way, and the perverted mouth, I hate."

PROVERBS 18:12
"Before destruction the heart of a man is haughty, but humility goes before honor."

PROVERBS 22:4
"The reward of humility and the fear of the LORD are riches, honor and life."

The Gate of Reuben/The Anti-Messiah Spirit

2 JOHN 7-9
"For many deceivers have gone out into the world, those who do not acknowledge Jesus Christ as coming in the flesh. This is the deceiver and the antichrist. Anyone who goes too far and does not abide in the teaching of the Christ, does not have God; the one who abides in the teaching, he has both the Father and the Son."

MATTHEW 24: 23-24
"Then if anyone says to you, 'Behold here is the Christ', or 'There he is', do not believe him. For false Christs and false prophets will arise and show great signs and wonders, so as to mislead, if possible even the elect."

JOHN 10:10-11
"The thief comes but to steal, and kill, and destroy. I came that they might have life and might have it abundantly."

MATTHEW 11:28-30
"Come to me, all you who are weary and heavy-laden, and I will give you rest. For my yoke is easy, and my load is light."

JOHN 15:18-20
"If the world hates you, know that it hated me before it hated you. If you were of the world the world would love its own; but because you are not of the world, but I chose you out of the world, therefore the world hates you. Remember the word that I said unto you, A slave is not greater than his master. If they persecuted me they will also persecute you;"

JOHN 16:1-3
"These things I have spoken to you, that you may be kept from stumbling. They will make you outcasts from the synagogue, but an hour is coming for everyone who kills you to think that he is offering service

to God. And these things they will do, because they have not known the Father or me."

MATTHEW 5:11-12
"Blessed are you when men cast insults at you, and persecute you, and say all kinds of evil against you falsely, on account of me. Rejoice, and be glad, for your reward in heaven is great, for so they persecuted the prophets who were before you."

2 CORINTHIANS 4:8-9
"...we are afflicted in every way, but not crushed; perplexed but not despairing, persecuted but not forsaken, struck down but not destroyed..."

MATTHEW 5:44a
"But I say to you, love your enemies, and pray for those who persecute you."

MARK 3:27
"But no one can enter the strong man's house and plunder his property unless he first bind the strong man, and then he will plunder his house."

ECCLESIASTES 1:9
"That which has been is that which will be, and that which has been done is that which will be done. So, there is nothing new under the sun."

The Gate of Gad/Spirit of Fear

2 TIMOTHY 1:7
"For God has not given us a spirit of timidity, but of power, and love, and discipline."

PSALM 34:4
"I sought the LORD, and He answered me. And delivered me from all of my fears."

PSALM 34:7

"The angel of the Lord encamps around those who fear Him, and rescues them."

PSALM 27:1-3

"The LORD is my light and my salvation; Whom shall I fear? The LORD is the defense of my life; Whom shall I dread? Though a host encamp against me, My heart will not fear, Though war arise against me, in spite of this I shall be confident."

PSALM 27:13

"I would have despaired unless I had believed that I would see the goodness of the LORD in the land of the living."

PSALM 56:3-4

"When I am afraid, I will put my trust in You. In God, whose word I praise, In God I have put my trust; I shall not be afraid."

PSALM 60:12

"Through God we shall do valiantly, and it is He who will tread down our adversaries."

PSALM 37:25

"I have been young, and now I am old; Yet I have not seen the righteous forsaken, or His descendants begging bread."

PSALM 23:4

"Even though I walk through the valley of the shadow of death, I fear no evil, for You are with me; Your rod and Your staff, they comfort me."

JOHN 14:27b

"Let not your heart be troubled, nor let it be fearful."

MATTHEW 6:34

"Therefore do not be anxious for tomorrow; for tomorrow will care for itself. Each day has enough trouble of its own."

PHILIPPIANS 4:6-7

"Be anxious for nothing, but in everything by prayer and supplication with thanksgiving let your requests be made known to God. And the peace of God which surpasses all comprehension shall guard your hearts and your minds in Christ Jesus."

The Gate of Asher/Spirit of Heaviness

ISAIAH 61:3a

"To grant those who mourn in Zion, giving them a garland instead of ashes, the oil of gladness instead of mourning. The mantle of praise instead of a spirit of fainting."

ISAIAH 35:10

"And the ransomed of the LORD will return, and come with joyful shouting unto Zion, with everlasting joy upon their heads. They will find gladness and joy, and sorrow and sighing will flee away."

PSALM 118:15

"The sound of joyful shouting and salvation is in the tents of the righteous; the right hand of the LORD does valiantly."

PSALM 97:12

"Be glad in the LORD, you righteous ones; and give thanks to His holy name."

PSALM 33:21

"For our heart rejoices in Him, because we trust in His holy name."

ISAIAH 55:12

"For you will go out with joy, and be led forth with peace, The mountains and the hills will break forth into shouts of joy before you, and all the trees of the field will clap their hands."

PSALM 68:3
"But let the righteous be glad; let them exult before God; Yes let them rejoice with gladness."

PSALM 30:11a
"You have turned for me my mourning into dancing; You have loosed my sackcloth and girded me with gladness..."

EPHESIANS 5:18-19
"And do not get drunk with wine, for that is dissipation, but be filled with the Spirit, speaking to one another in psalms, and hymns and spiritual songs, singing and making melody with your heart to the Lord."

ROMANS 14:17
"...for the kingdom of God is not eating and drinking, but righteousness, and peace, and joy in the Holy Spirit."

NEHEMIAH 8:10b
"Do not be grieved for the joy of the LORD is your strength."

PHILIPPIANS 4:4
"Rejoice in the LORD always, again I will say, rejoice!"

The Gate of Zebulon/Familiar Spirits

ISAIAH 1:16
"Wash yourselves, make yourselves clean; Remove the evil of your deeds from My sight. Cease to do evil."

ISAIAH 1:4
"Alas, sinful nation. People weighed down with iniquity, Offspring of evildoers, Sons who act corruptly. They have abandoned the LORD. They have despised the Holy One of Israel. They have turned away from Him. Where will you be stricken again, as you continue in your rebellion?"

DEUTERONOMY 18:9
"When you enter the land which the LORD your God gives you, you shall not learn to imitate the detestable things of those nations..."

DEUTERONOMY 7:26
"And you shall not bring an abomination into your house, and like it come under the ban (curse); you shall utterly detest it and you shall utterly abhor it, for it is something banned."

1 PETER 2:16
"Act as free men, and do not use your freedom as a covering for evil, but use it as bond slaves of God."

ROMANS 6:22
"But now having been freed from sin and enslaved to God, you derive your benefit, resulting in sanctification, and the outcome, eternal life."

REVELATION 21:8
"But the cowardly and unbelieving and abominable and murderers and immoral persons and sorcerers and idolaters and all liars, their part will be in the lake that burns with fire and brim-stone, which is the second death."

MATTHEW 12:43-45
"Now when the unclean spirit goes out of a man, it passes through waterless places, seeking rest, and does not find it. Then it says, 'I will return to my house from which I came', and when it comes, it finds it unoccupied, swept, and put in order. Then it goes, and takes along with it seven other spirits more wicked than itself, and they go in and they live there; and the last state of that man becomes worse than the first. This is the way it will also be with this evil generation."

The Gate of Naphtali/Spirit of Jealousy

EPHESIANS 4:1-3
"I, therefore, the prisoner of the Lord, entreat you to walk in a manner worthy of the calling, with which you have been called, with all humility and gentleness, with patience, showing forbearance to one another in love, being diligent to preserve the unity of the Spirit in the bond of peace."

PHILIPPIANS 2:3-4
"Do nothing from selfishness or empty conceit, but with humility of mind let each of you regard one another as more important than himself; do not merely look out for your own personal interests but also for the interests of others."

PHILIPPIANS 4:11-13
"Not that I speak from want; for I have learned to be content in whatever circumstances I am. I know how to get along with humble means, and I also know how to live in prosperity; in every and any circumstance I have learned the secret of being filled and going hungry, both of having abundance and suffering need. I can do all things through Him who strengthens me."

PROVERBS 22:24-25
"Do not associate with a man given to anger; or go with a hot-tempered man, lest you learn his ways, and find a snare for yourself."

PROVERBS 15:18
"A hot-tempered man stirs up strife, but the slow to anger pacifies contention."

PROVERBS 15:28
"The heart of the righteous ponders how to answer, but the mouth of the wicked pours out wicked things."

PROVERBS 15:1
"A gentle answer turns away wrath, but a harsh word stirs up anger."

PROVERBS 14:29
"He who is slow to anger has great understanding, but he who is quick-tempered exalts folly."

EPHESIANS 4:26
"Be angry, and yet do not sin. Do not let the sun go down on your anger and do not give the devil an opportunity."

EPHESIANS 4:31-32
"Let all bitterness, and wrath and anger and clamor and slander be put away from you, along with all malice and be kind to one another, tenderhearted, forgiving each other, just as God in Christ has forgiven you."

PSALM 145:8
"The Lord is gracious and merciful; Slow to anger and great in loving-kindness."

1 CORINTHIANS 13:4-8a
"Love is patient, love is kind, and is not jealous, love does not brag and is not arrogant, does not act unbecomingly, it does not seek its own, is not provoked, does not take into account a wrong suffered, does not rejoice with unrighteousness but rejoices with the truth; bears all things, believes all things, hopes all things, and endures all things, love never fails."

The Gate of Dan/Spirit of Bondage

2 CORINTHIANS 4:3-4
"And even if our gospel is veiled, it is veiled to those who are perishing, in whose case the god of this world has blinded the minds of

the unbelieving, that they might not see the light of the gospel of the glory of Christ, who is the image of God."

MATTHEW 6:12; 14-15

"And forgive us our debts as we have also forgiven our debtors. For if you forgive men for their transgressions, your heavenly Father will also forgive you: But if you do not forgive men, then your Father will not forgive your transgressions."

MARK 11:24-25

"Therefore I say to you, all things for which you pray and ask, believe that you have received them, and they shall be granted you. And whenever you stand praying, forgive, if you have anything against anyone; so that your Father also who is in heaven may forgive you your transgressions. But if you do not forgive neither will your Father who is in heaven forgive your transgressions."

PSALM 66:18

"If I regard wickedness in my heart, The Lord will not hear."

ISAIAH 61:1

"The Spirit of the Lord GOD is upon me, because the LORD has anointed me, to bring good news to the afflicted; He has sent me to bind up the brokenhearted, to proclaim liberty to captives, and freedom to prisoners."

ROMANS 6:10-12

"For the death that He died, He died to sin, once for all; but the life that He lives, He lives to God. Even so consider yourselves to be dead to sin, but alive to God in Christ Jesus. Therefore do not let sin reign in your mortal body that you should obey its lusts."

PSALM 119-133

"Establish my footsteps in Your word, and do not let any iniquity have dominion over me."

PSALM 119:11
"Your word I have treasured in my heart, that I may not sin against You."

EPHESIANS 5:18-19
"And do not get drunk with wine for that is dissipation, but be filled with the Spirit, speaking to one another with psalms and hymns, and spiritual songs, singing and making melody with your heart to the Lord."

1 PETER 4:1
"Therefore, since Christ has suffered in the flesh, arm yourselves also with the same purpose, because he who has suffered in the flesh has ceased from sin."

WORKS CITED

Bolen, Todd. 2008. "The Acoustics of Mounts Gerizim and Ebal." *Bibleplaces.com Blog*, December 8: http://blog.bibleplaces.com/2008/12/acoustics-of-mounts-gerizim-and-ebal.html.

Savard, Liberty. 1993. "Shattering your Strongholds." In *Shattering your Strongholds*, by Liberty Savard. Bridge-Logos Publishing.

Snyder, Michael, interview by Jim & Lori Bakker. 2016. *The Jim Bakker Show, PTL Television Network* (August 25).

Strong, James. n.d. *Blue Letter Bible.* Accessed September 11, 2016. www.blbclassic.org/lang/lexicon/Lexicon.cfm?Strongs=H8176&t=KJV.

Tenney, Tommy. 1999. In *God's Dream Team: A Call to Corporate Unity*, by Tommy Tenney. Ventura, CA: Regal Books.

CPSIA information can be obtained
at www.ICGtesting.com
Printed in the USA
LVOW07s2001020517

532928LV00002BA/466/P